RETIREMENT GUIDE

RETIREMENT GUIDE

An overall plan for a comfortable future

Henry S. Hunnisett
Denise Lamaute, J.D., LL.M.(TAX)

Self-Counsel Press Inc.
a subsidiary of
International Self-Counsel Press Ltd.
Canada   U.S.A.
(Printed in Canada)

Copyright © 1990 by Self-Counsel Press Inc.

All rights reserved.

No part of this book may be reproduced or transmitted in any form by any means without permission in writing from the publisher, except by a reviewer who may quote brief passages in a review.

Printed in Canada

First edition: March, 1990

Canadian Cataloguing in Publication Data

Hunnisett, Henry S., 1914-
    Retirement Guide

    (Self-counsel retirement series)
    ISBN 0-88908-926-4

    1. Retirement. 2. Retirement income. I. Lamaute, Denise. II. Title. III. Series.
HQ1062.H86 1990   646.7'9   C90-091083-6

Self-Counsel Press Inc.
a subsidiary of
International Self-Counsel Press Ltd.
Head and Editorial Office
1481 Charlotte Road
North Vancouver, British Columbia V7J 1H1

U.S. Address
1704 N. State Street
Bellingham, Washington   98225

CONTENTS

PREFACE — xvii
- a. What will it bring? — xvii
- b. Why is this? — xvii
- c. Three requirements for happiness — xviii
- d. Married or single — xviii
- e. Your responsibilities — xix

1 ARE YOU READY TO RETIRE? — 1
- a. Accepting change — 2
- b. A new life cycle — 3
- c. The time dilemma — 4
- d. Are you ready for leisure? — 5
- e. The choice is yours — 6
- f. The test — 7
- g. Early retirement — 10

2 THE PSYCHOLOGICAL REACTION TO RETIREMENT — 12
- a. The shock of job withdrawal — 12
  1. Loss of the familiar — 13
  2. Loss of job satisfaction — 13
  3. Loss of identity — 14
- b. Lost goals — 15
- c. The loss of work place companionship — 15

	d.	Variety — the spice of life	16
	e.	Financial concerns	17
	f.	On the bottom? take the upturn!	17
3	**FOR YOUR HAPPINESS AND PEACE OF MIND**		19
	a.	Identify your problems and act	19
	b.	Is retirement justified?	20
	c.	Financial security	21
	d.	The importance of interests and activities	21
	e.	Attitude	22
	f.	Religion	22
	g.	The promised solutions	23
4	**CHOOSE FROM A SMORGASBORD OF ACTIVITIES**		24
	a.	Social activities	25
	b.	Join the club	26
	c.	Physical fitness	27
	d.	Sports	28
		1. Tennis	28
		2. Curling	29
		3. Golf	30
		4. Swimming	31
		5. Hunting	31
		6. Fishing	32

		7. Boating	33
		8. Walking and hiking	33
		9. Bowling	34
		10. Shuffleboard	34
	e.	Entertainment	34
	f.	Hobbies	35
		1. Woodworking	36
		2. Gardening	36
		3. Photography	37
		4. Bird watching	38
	g.	Continuing education	38
	h.	Libraries and reading	39
	i.	Politics	40
	j.	Creative activities	41
	k.	Travel	42
		1. Take advantage of discounts	42
		2. The trailer and the recreational vehicle	42
	l.	Volunteer work	44
	m.	For self-starters and leaders	45
5	**PERSONAL AND FAMILY RELATIONSHIPS IN RETIREMENT**		46
	a.	Replace employment contacts	46
	b.	The strains of retirement on marriage	47
		1. A wife's independent life	48

       2. Who will be in charge?   49
       3. Don't spoil it!   49
       4. Both can benefit   50
   c. Your family   51
   d. Family relationships   52
   e. You become the receiver   53
   f. Grandchildren   53
   g. Sons- or daughters-in-law   54
   h. Friends, old and new   55

6 THE SINGLE PERSON   57
   a. The opportunities   58
       1. Organized activities   58
       2. Financial concerns   59
   b. To love and be loved   59
   c. Should you marry?   60
   d. Living alone   61
   e. Living a satisfactory life   62

7 MONEY MATTERS   63
   a. Calculate your total joint income   64
   b. Your income checklist   65
   c. How do you spend your income?   69
       1. Payroll deductions   70

	2. How to calculate the cost of home ownership	70
	3. Personal expenses	74
	4. Automobile costs and depreciation	74
	d. The final list	76
8	**ESTIMATING RETIREMENT INCOME**	**78**
	a. Maintaining your standard of living	78
	b. Assessing your needs	80
	c. Consider inflation	83
	d. Planning for the unexpected	84
	e. Conclusion	84
9	**YOUR COST OF LIVING IN RETIREMENT**	**86**
	a. Income tax responsibilities	86
	b. Do not let them lapse!	87
	c. Your home	88
	d. Eating for health and pleasure	88
	e. Clothing	90
	f. Entertainment	90
	g. Vacations and travel	90
	h. Eliminate installment payments	91
	i. Medical coverage	91
	j. Transportation	92
	k. Bank charges	93
	l. Evaluate each expenditure again	93

10 HOW TO INCREASE YOUR RETIREMENT INCOME 95

   a. Safe investments 96
      1. Savings accounts 97
      2. Money market accounts and money market funds 97
      3. Certificates of deposit 98
      4. Federal Treasury investments 99
   b. Mutual funds 101
   c. Stocks and bonds 103
   d. Other investments 104

11 COPING WITH INFLATION 106

   a. The squeeze — rising living costs, lower income 106
   b. Interest rates 107
   c. Investments with inflation hedge 109
      1. Real estate 109
      2. Art, jewels, antiques, coins, and stamps 110
   d. Reverse mortgages 111
   e. "The hedge" 111

12 SOCIAL SECURITY 113

   a. Eligibility 113
   b. Family entitlement 114
   c. Working after retirement 115
   d. Early retirement 115

		e. Accurate account	116
		f. Taxes	117
		g. Medicare	117
13	**PUT YOUR AFFAIRS IN ORDER**		118
	a.	Legal matters	118
		1. Power of attorney	119
		2. Why have a will?	120
		3. Your will	121
		4. The living will	122
	b.	Funeral plans — The unpopular topic	123
	c.	Think of your spouse!	124
		1. The cost of dying	125
		2. Estate tax planning	125
		3. Leaving property to your spouse	127
		4. Joint tenancy	127
		5. Private or industrial pension plans	128
		6. Life insurance	128
		7. Remarriage	129
14	**CHOOSING YOUR RETIREMENT HOME**		131
	a.	What should it provide?	131
	b.	What should it cost?	133
	c.	Evaluating a retirement home	134
	d.	Making the choice	135

	1. Renting	135
	2. Purchasing	136
e.	Condominiums	138
	1. Operation and cost sharing	139
	2. Purchasing	140
	3. Owner's responsibilities and costs	141
	4. Some advantages of condominium ownership	142
	5. Some disadvantages of ownership	143
	6. What to watch for	144
f.	Cooperative apartments	144
g.	Rental apartments	145
h.	Mobile or manufactured homes	146
	1. What are they like?	146
	2. Choosing the location	148
	3. Financing	149
	4. What to watch for	150
i.	The retirement community	151
j.	When more help is required	151
	1. Retirement homes	152
	2. Choosing the home	154
	3. The life care retirement community	155
k.	Caring for an elderly relative or spouse	156

15	**WHERE WILL YOU LIVE?**	158
	a. Financial considerations	158
	b. Possibility of employment	159
	c. A better climate	160
	d. Move to a foreign country with caution!	161
	1. What can you gain or lose?	161
	2. Possible language difficulties	162
	3. The best of both worlds	162
	e. Different views of moving	163
	f. Try it out first!	163
16	**YOUR HEALTH AND RETIREMENT**	165
	a. Find something to do	166
	b. Maintaining good health	167
	1. Exercise	167
	2. Diet	168
	3. Alcohol	168
	4. Smoking	169
	5. Sex	170
	c. Enter the doctor	171
	1. Illness	172
	2. Drugs and medicines	173
	3. Doctor-patient problems	174
	4. Conclusions	174

17 MAKING YOUR FINAL PLAN 175
    a. Set your goals 175
    b. The new value of time 176
    c. Do not believe it! 176
    d. Be active 177
    e. Love continues 178
    f. A life with quality 178

APPENDIXES

1 Checklist for retiring 181

2 Resources for retired people 183

LIST OF SAMPLES

#1	Gross income while employed 199-	68
#2	Estimated automobile expenses	76
#3	How the money was spent	77

LIST OF TABLES

#1	Life expectancy	82
#2	Impact of inflation	83
#3	Property subject to estate taxes	126

LIST OF WORKSHEETS

#1	Retirement expenditures	81
#2	Estimating your annual retirement income	85

PREFACE

a. WHAT WILL IT BRING?

The demands of the job have been left behind, the alarm clock has been sent to the Goodwill, and a steady stream of social security checks, perhaps supplemented by additional sources, brings in a secure income. There is time to relax and soak up the sun in quiet contentment. It must be the ideal happy life, or so conventional wisdom would have you believe. But if you talk to a broad sample of retired people, a different picture emerges. Some, it is true, are very happy and they have never enjoyed themselves more. But many are unhappy and wish they could return to work and the life they knew during their working years.

Something has gone wrong. People who are released from their jobs at an age when they are still physically active and are provided with an income that enables them to live in comfort are supposed to have an automatic passport to happiness. Obviously this has not always been the experience.

b. WHY IS THIS?

Has there been a misunderstanding? Is more left behind with the job than is often realized? One day you have both a busy day and a day's pay: the next day you have neither.

This is a drastic change. There are questions to answer, decisions to make, and much to replace. Will your expected income enable you to maintain your present lifestyle? Will you be able to afford those new things that you hoped would put zest into your life? Passing those hours spent at work in an enjoyable manner may be more difficult than expected, yet happiness may depend on it. There is no longer a superior to direct and help. You must recognize the problems and find the solutions yourself. Those who succeed usually enjoy life as much or more than ever. Those who fail are often bored, miserable, and resentful.

c. THREE REQUIREMENTS FOR HAPPINESS

At any stage of life there are three requirements for happiness: the first is sufficient income to support a satisfactory lifestyle, the second is to love and be loved, and the third is to feel that your life is being used in a manner that fulfills those needs and goals that you consider desirable.

The purpose of this guide is to eliminate guesswork and assist you to achieve this satisfying life. It clearly explains many of the financial benefits to which you may be entitled, some of which you may not be aware. Pitfalls are pointed out and solutions offered for avoiding them. How to determine housing needs and the possible advantages of retirement communities are discussed. Some of the ways others have found helpful in making a new and happy life are reviewed.

d. MARRIED OR SINGLE

Because most people who retire are married, and as retirement often puts new and serious strains on the husband/wife relationship, this topic is given extensive consideration. Recognizing that there is a growing number of women of retirement age in the work force, this guide is written for both women and men. Both you and your spouse should read this text, no matter which of you is retiring, not only to help yourself, but also to assist you in understanding your partner's side of the change, and in recognizing when help is required and how it should be given.

As the number of single people, particularly women, who are retiring is increasing, there is a new enlarged section dealing with their situation as well.

e. YOUR RESPONSIBILITIES

The key to a successful retirement is twofold. First, accept the idea that you can make this a happy time of your life, and, second, realize that you will have to work at it to make it so. *You can make a satisfactory life for yourself in your later years, but it is your own efforts that make it: society just provides the environment.* There will be many who fail to find satisfaction, some for lack of knowledge, others for lack of trying. Failure now can be the final disaster, success the crowning achievement of your life. Success will not only help you, but will take the strain of worry from your family and friends, enabling them to see you as a valued friend or family member. Your example will show what these years can be and will leave them with a cherished memory of you.

Note: The facts included in this book have been obtained from sources we believe to be reliable but they are not guaranteed. In view of the frequency with which changes occur, the reader is cautioned to use them only as a guideline for thought. Before taking action, you should check the facts to make sure they are accurate. This is especially so in matters of law or government policy, both of which are subject to frequent changes.

1
ARE YOU READY TO RETIRE?

Individuals differ in their expectations of retirement. Those who have found their work boring or stressful may think that leaving it will automatically create a better life. Others who have liked their work may fear that retirement will not be as enjoyable. Both may be unrealistic, for their views are based on an inaccurate understanding of the obligations and opportunities and what each person can and must do to create a new, different, and happy life. This could result in improper preparation and planning.

It is difficult to form an accurate mental picture of retirement before it arrives. Perhaps the best comparison can be made with a period of convalescence after an illness when an immediate return to work is forbidden. Even this is different because there was an end to it in sight. How did you find the time sitting around home? Were there things you could do indefinitely that you really wanted to do, or were you longing to get back to work? Did you ever consider what it would be like if you could never return to work again?

All you have to relate to are your past experiences, and the closest thing to retirement is weekend and vacation time. But this is not a true standard for comparison, for a weekend provides a welcome break that is too short to get bored and is usually required for personal and family matters and necessary rest and recreation. Vacations are not fair standards either, for these are planned well ahead for concentrated pleasure that is often expensive and that you can afford, and often endure, for only short periods at well-spaced intervals. Retirement will be unlike either of these experiences.

a. ACCEPTING CHANGE

The next step in making satisfaction a reality is to accept that there must be a great many changes in your life. Any fears you have about retirement are really just paper tigers, much greater in imagination than reality. Once faced, they lack substance and fade away.

Everyone dislikes change. It means the loss of the familiar and the introduction of the unknown. However, the changes that come with retirement are different in one very important respect from those that were forced on you by work or other obligations. You may now choose those you will enjoy. Look on it as the means of release from the old bonds and an opportunity to build a new life according to your chosen plan.

Now that you have an understanding of the very different factors that affect your retirement planning, you are ready to start building that life. But, before you begin, let's review some important points:

(a) Forget the old responsibilities of job, family, and earning an income. Accept that that stage is past and the book is closed. Concentrate on making the days ahead happy and useful for you and your spouse.

(b) Realize the changed position in which your retirement may place your spouse. Prior to this, much of your life was spent apart and your work done in different fields, often without consulting each other. But now you spend much of your time together. These are difficult changes and much friction can result. It will require understanding and cooperation, but it can be planned successfully. It is most important because living with a happy spouse will make this time that you will spend together so much more enjoyable.

(c) Understand any restrictions or demands placed on you by your health. The maintenance of good health is more important than ever before and you need the advice and assistance of your doctor. If you have not had a complete physical examination, don't put it off any longer.

(d) Develop a positive attitude: you *are* going to enjoy retirement and you will not succumb to lethargy, but will seek out those things you require for satisfaction.

(e) Welcome change — it is the ingredient on which the whole success of retirement depends. Only through change can the old be replaced by the new.

b. A NEW LIFE CYCLE

An automatic washing machine performs by going through a series of distinct cycles: washing, rinsing, and spin-drying. When one cycle has finished, the next runs until it has completed its function and then is followed by its successor. Similarly, life begins with infancy and is followed by childhood, growth, education, and experiences in human relations. These are the necessary preparations for the next and longest cycle — your working life, during which you devote the best part of your day to employment in or outside the home.

The day you retire you end the lifestyle that began the day you started school, many years ago! During the intervening years, your schedule was generally set by others. As a child at school, you observed the routine laid down by the teacher; at home you followed your parents' rules. When you became an adult with your own family and work responsibilities, more demands were put on you. Employment either provided for or contributed to your support and that of your family and laid the financial base for retirement. You have given the best part of your life and strength to your work obligations. Now, on the day of your retirement, this cycle grinds to a halt. It is finished, period.

When the door closes after you for the last time on the day of retirement, your previous lifestyle will be left behind with the job. It will be filed away with the closed records of your past employment. You can't take it with you because that life was job-oriented and the job no longer exists for you. You are now on your own and must build a life completely different from that which you have been leading.

You have begun a new life cycle. You are released from the obligation of daily work and now have the right to use each and every day as you wish. It is a new game with a new team, played on a new field. Points are scored for making entirely new goals from those that previously counted.

c. THE TIME DILEMMA

Anticipating what time will mean after retirement is difficult. It is common to think that retirement will simply be an endless series of holidays; many people never think deeply enough about it beforehand to see the fallacy in this. When every day becomes a holiday, the appeal is lost.

So it is with leisure time, when it becomes a 24-hour-a-day, 7-days-a-week continuous lifetime supply. Unless much of this leisure time is filled with activities of interest and some activities that include obligations requiring some effort, it becomes a boring, frustrating hell.

Think for a moment about time and how your value of it has changed over the years. As a young person, you probably considered it a renewable resource. If you made a mistake or failed in some endeavor, there was always time to try again. Your dreams were all still possible but, as the years went by, there were more candles on the birthday cake and certain things turned out to be final. Patterns unlikely to be reversible developed and limitations became evident. Time began to take on greater value. Frequently, events of a serious nature drive it home — the passing of friends and contemporaries, graying hair, illnesses, growing children.

The solution to this problem is easy to see, but more difficult to put into effect. Often you must work as hard at enjoying retirement as you did to earn your living. For some, the answer is to continue working and find another job. But most of us must face the reality that our retirement system is designed to get us *out* of the work force.

d. ARE YOU READY FOR LEISURE?

Before you are faced with imminent retirement, the thought of having unlimited time at your disposal probably seems like Utopia. However, unless you have prepared, when retirement arrives it may not be as delightful as you expected. You are so conditioned to working full days, generally against a time schedule, that subconsciously you will expect it to continue. For years you have strived to arrive on time, complete jobs on time, keep appointments, and do so much per hour. Regardless of what your job was, time was a steady master and you were the puppet on its strings.

Nice as it is to be released from this bondage, you may find yourself unprepared for leisure. Subconsciously, you may feel that there must be something you should be doing, somewhere you should be going, and you may feel guilty for having so much free time. The change is so sudden that it is difficult to relax and enjoy this new-found freedom.

There are no standard "rules" of how to best use your time. No two people are exactly alike; some require an almost frenzied schedule, even in retirement, while others will be fully satisfied with a rocking chair and slippers. This is the reason that it is continually emphasized throughout this book that you must suit *your* needs and build a program that fills *your* personal requirements.

e. THE CHOICE IS YOURS

Perhaps for the first time you and your spouse, if you have one, can be perfectly selfish. The responsibilities to your job and family have been fulfilled, and your only obligation is to yourselves, so start out to do all those things you have been unable to do for the lack of time.

Start by listing all the things you enjoy. There may be much icing here, but that is good, for you are entitled to it. Then think of other things your personality may require.

Others may attempt to influence your choice, feeling that you should enjoy the things they do. Consider their suggestions but make your own choices, for no one else can really know what will be of most value to you.

The daily activity of making your living has made a most important contribution to your life. Dr. Bronowski in *The Ascent of Man* states: "The most powerful drive in the ascent of man is his pleasure in his own skill. He loves to do what he does well, and having done it well, he loves to do it better."

You must replace this essential part of your life with something just as satisfying. You will want some continuing responsibility that you are obligated to perform (the word "obligated" is important) and some activity in which you are very involved as essential ingredients in a replacement for work.

f. THE TEST

To determine how well you are prepared, answer the following five questions carefully and honestly. Writing the answers helps in this respect, for in answering verbally, it is too easy to let things slip by with the observation, "I guess I know that."

Make a list of any questions you could not answer properly. Knowing what your questions are will make it simpler to recognize the answers as you read through this guide.

(a) *Am I in a financial position to live in a manner that will be satisfactory to me and my spouse?* You should first know your total present household income and what parts will continue or cease. You should know not only how your income has been spent, but how the total has been divided among the major categories such as food, housing, medical, etc. You must also have an accurate estimate of your retirement income and to get this may require some investigation. Then, estimate what changes in expenses can be expected. Many of the expenditures listed above may continue, but there will be important changes.

Deducting any reduction and adding any anticipated increases will provide an estimated cost of living in retirement. Comparing the estimated expenditure with the income will indicate what your financial position will be; essential information to make a realistic retirement plan. Chapters 7 to 10 will provide detailed assistance in working out these matters.

(b) *Will I be able to use my time in a manner that will make life enjoyable?* How well you are prepared to use your time in a satisfactory manner is something in which many deceive themselves. There is a tendency to think that things will just automatically come along to occupy this new daily eight- or nine-hour stretch of time in an enjoyable manner, but that is unlikely to happen. A few interests occupying a short time each week is not enough. It is essential that you have interests and/or activities started that can be expanded to take up the slack. If not, you must add new activities to do so. How you succeed in handling this challenge may determine the quality of life in the coming years. Chapter 4 discusses the opportunities.

(c) *Am I mentally prepared to accept the change from a working life to retirement?* Everyone has a self image. Our society values work as a virtue. Your employment has been an important part of your image, both to yourself and others. You have lived up to this demand, paid your way, and have to feel that it has contributed to your worth and status. After retirement, some erroneously continue to use the working world's standards and by so doing, see themselves as without further value. Some even give up and pass away.

It is essential that you realize that your past accomplishments cannot be taken away, and to also accept that that chapter is finished. There are now new standards of value in which paid employment is not included. This is not an easy transition, yet accepting it is necessary for contentment and peace of mind in retirement. These matters are investigated in chapter 3.

(d) *Do my plans take into account the wishes, interests, and welfare of my spouse so that we will be able to live happily together?* During the working years, many of the decisions affecting all aspects of life were dictated by employment and were accepted by both spouses. After retirement, with those demands gone, each spouse may desire to fill the void with things of personal interest but which may not be enjoyed by the other partner. Each should understand the other's needs and wishes and be willing to compromise when necessary to maintain harmony. This is considered in chapter 5.

(e) *Will my present home help or hinder my life in retirement? Are there good reasons to remain, or to go elsewhere?* Your home and its location will play an important part in every aspect of life. Those things that were important when working and raising a family may be disadvantages after retirement. Its suitability should be seriously considered. The following questions must be answered (see chapters 14 and 15):

- Will it be too expensive?
- Will its location enable you to reach those interests you desire?
- Is it convenient for family and friends to visit?
- Will it be a source of satisfaction?
- Would a home designed and located specifically for retirement be a better source of new interests for you?

g. EARLY RETIREMENT

The number of persons taking early retirement is increasing. Obviously, they expect that it will lead to a better life. For this to be realized, there must be sufficient income to support the new life they seek. Observation reveals that the majority have correctly assessed their financial positions and are free of money problems.

There is a second requirement, and in this, many have not been successful. Those who retire for a specific reason, to get into a business or occupation which they believe will provide a much better life or to carry out a well-prepared, fulfilling plan for their lives are usually happy. But others, who retire just to escape the job without a plan to replace it with a better life, not realizing that this could be dull and unhappy, often wish that they had remained where they were.

Leaving a job at or near retirement time is usually an irrevocable step. Your decision will be a personal one and should be made only after a careful understanding of what the step will mean, and how you and your spouse will find life if you take that step.

If you wish to take early retirement, make a realistic assessment of your position using the questions listed above. If this reveals that you are not ready, there are options:

(a) Remain employed until your preparations are completed

(b) Try to work out job improvements with your employer

(c) Find a better job

(d) Grin and bear it until you are ready.

There should be many more years of life, but it is your responsibility to make them happy ones. Spending a little time in preparation may be the key. It will be well worth the effort.

2
THE PSYCHOLOGICAL REACTION TO RETIREMENT

A group of retired people with whom I was working filled out a questionnaire that was designed to reveal how they were enjoying retirement. Twenty-two of the twenty-five indicated difficulty in accepting and enjoying their new-found leisure because they were plagued by thoughts that something was "wrong." There was no reason why they should have these thoughts, but they did, and the thoughts would not disappear by simply being told to go away. Unwarranted fears can monopolize your thinking, become absorbing obsessions, and make your life miserable. Retirement is a fertile seedbed for this problem.

This chapter considers some common causes of this condition. Once the causes are understood, it is possible to see the solution.

a. THE SHOCK OF JOB WITHDRAWAL

The change from long-term, full-time employment to retirement is too great for most people to experience without suffering some kind of reaction. How serious your reaction is depends on three things: the satisfaction you derived from your job, the preparation you have made for retirement, and your ability to cope with a change of this magnitude.

The reaction can range from a simple feeling of being lost, uprooted, unwanted, bewildered, and alone in a strange world to breakdown and mental illness which, fortunately, is uncommon.

1. Loss of the familiar

Everyone experiences difficulty when faced with the loss of the familiar. The more important and long-standing the subject the more difficult the transition. Consequently, the loss of your long-term employment will rate high on the problem scale; the daily routine has been torn away leaving a great gap.

The years of repetition wore deep grooves and your life slipped along easily in them without the need for guidance; it will be difficult to change direction. You must now learn to chart your own course, which may require persistence.

The job was the hinge on which your life was hung; it determined which way that hinge could swing and what could be permitted in the time remaining after working hours. You couldn't accept anything that would place your job in jeopardy, particularly as you grew older and jobs became more difficult to find. Your strength was used to fill the job's demands, and only the surplus was available for personal purposes. Your home was located to be accessible to your job and your family could be uprooted and moved to a new location when the job required it. It was your "security blanket" and you are bound to feel insecure without it.

2. Loss of job satisfaction

The satisfaction a job provides is not usually appreciated until it is gone. Often, the paycheck is considered to be the main source of satisfaction, yet if you lose your job, it soon becomes apparent that there is much more to employment than money alone.

This may come as a surprise, especially if you considered your job as difficult or unpleasant and longed to be able to give it up. Only after you do so is it obvious that the strain and the annoyances that provided mental activity in themselves are certainly preferable to boredom.

Retirement takes the pleasure of work from you; now it is essential to find alternative sources of satisfaction. It does not seem reasonable that there should be so much difficulty once you are given this opportunity, but there is. Your mind has been living with a comfortable pattern, the road familiar, the direction clear. This is wiped out, and, just at the time when unclouded thought and effort is required to set the new direction, the shock of it all seems to confuse and stop all motion.

3. Loss of identity

People identify with their jobs; they think of themselves as machinists, accountants, executives, teachers, etc. Your job identity is an important part of the mental image you have of yourself. By retirement you may have accumulated seniority or risen to a position of importance that earns deference and respect from others.

Before retirement, these things are of real value to any individual who enjoys them. But after retirement, all these will vanish! It is a shock to realize that the attributes that were considered personally yours, and which were the reasons for your importance, have been taken away and given to your successor. You stand outside the door; inside the work goes on as before, but without your help. You are no longer needed, nor are you the person you thought you were and that important identity has been lost. You may be bewildered, unsure of who you are or what you should be doing.

b. LOST GOALS

The feeling that you have a purpose in life with a particular goal to reach is essential to a fulfilled life. Part of life's goal for a working person is usually the attainment of some position in the future; for a homemaker it is a well-run home and the achievement of a plan for the children.

Doing your job and raising your family have been the main goals that supplied purpose to life. Now, both those goals have been reached and you may be left feeling that there is no longer any reason to continue. It is a depressing thought, and the empty days may come and go with no apparent reason for their existence.

c. THE LOSS OF WORK PLACE COMPANIONSHIP

One of the basic human pleasures and needs is companionship, which a job often provides as the people you work with become good friends. In addition, your colleagues provide many other benefits: they will discuss your problems with you and provide support when troubles come; they do not hesitate to bring you back into line when you are off the beam or are worrying unnecessarily; if you develop a swelled head, they cut you down to size. All this will be missed and may contribute to a feeling of loneliness, one of the most deeply felt problems of older people.

A group of men discussing changes that retirement had brought to their lives agreed they had experienced a very noticeable and unexpected difference in the attitude of their old business friends. When they left work, they had realized and accepted that they would not be welcome back, but had expected their colleagues to continue their friendships. They felt that these friendships were built on mutual enjoyment of each other's company, and it was a shock to find that they quickly faded after retirement. In fact, the friendships arose from proximity and their value in the work place; once these no longer existed, new friendships took their places.

There is another aspect more difficult to understand: those still working tend to consider a retired person to be as much an outsider as someone who has quit and gone to work for a competitor. Perhaps this change of attitude is due to an understanding that retired people must develop a new lifestyle, for they have stepped into another world.

d. VARIETY — THE SPICE OF LIFE

After a day at work, returning home is anticipated with pleasure. But spending all your time at home can be boring. After a demanding but absorbing daily routine, a succession of empty days can be devastating.

The job's roots spread out in many directions, thereby contacting and bringing back nourishment from many sources. When there is nothing to take the place of the daily trip to work, it is too easy just to stay at home, all day and all night, and this frequently happens. Nothing can contribute more toward boredom.

During your working years, you are forced into the mainstream of life by job and family, but now it is easy to avoid involvement. The stream is still flowing and, while you need not venture out into the rapids, there are many suitable areas, calmer but wonderful, waiting to be discovered. Get out and recapture the variety.

e. FINANCIAL CONCERNS

A steady job provides security with its paycheck; haven't you known since you started that you must work to live? It is difficult to make your subconscious mind believe otherwise. Will the income from social security, pensions, and other sources be safe? Will your income be adequate? Will inflation continue and will it lead to financial problems?

While no one knows what will happen in the future, there are some practical steps you can take to secure yourself financially in retirement. Again, planning is the key. (See chapters 7 through 12.)

f. ON THE BOTTOM? TAKE THE UPTURN!

There is good reason to be apprehensive about retirement, but it doesn't mean that part of your life need be an empty and frustrating experience. Retirement is a personal experience. At one end of the spectrum are those who have prepared and, while they may have experienced some unexpected reactions, on the whole they are getting along well. At the opposite end are those who were completely unaware of what was coming; they are unpleasantly surprised and many of them will be among those who promptly sink into oblivion.

Most people, however, are between these two scenarios. They probably expected life to be something like it was on weekends and vacations, so the actual experience is a shock. "Retirement shock" has become a common phrase, with good reason. People who experience it are bewildered and drifting. They have no goal or purpose; they want something to fill the void, yet know neither what it is, nor where to find it. Rank, status, and identity have gone; they are unrecognized and unnecessary. But it may be just the darkest hour before dawn; there is no way to go but up, and it is up to you to change direction.

You don't have to make the turn unassisted. If you are scraping the bottom, now is the time to assess your attitude and make up your mind that this is enough, that you *will* take the future in hand and find the way to enjoy the rest of your life. Read on for some helpful ideas to get you started.

3

FOR YOUR HAPPINESS AND PEACE OF MIND

a. IDENTIFY YOUR PROBLEMS AND ACT

Among the major problems you may face in retirement are unhappiness and boredom. Identify the problems, and then understand and tackle them. Some problems may be handled by simply understanding, rationalizing, and putting them in perspective to reduce them from their imagined to their real size.

If action is required, take it at once, for delay only causes unnecessary worry. Do what you can, then stop worrying. Try to concentrate on something else, preferably something enjoyable. Undesirable thoughts tend to lose their strength and fade away if they aren't called upon. Another ally is time — the great healer — for its passing dulls the sting and allows solutions to take shape.

Once a problem is identified, you may not be able to solve it in one step, but often a partial solution leads to another. Do as much as you can, then accept the final reality and resolve to live with it. Do not permit it to ruin your life. In the case of those changes that you just do not like, such as the loss of importance, remember, THERE IS NO REAL PROBLEM. THE DISTRESS IS CAUSED ONLY BY THE WAY IN WHICH YOU ARE REACTING TO IT.

It is perfectly normal to have such feelings, and they are not easy to chase away, but keep in mind that it is only your *reaction* that is causing the problem. Most of the psychological problems have no real substance and, if put in perspective, disappear. If some are real and persist, don't despair, there are solutions for them all.

b. IS RETIREMENT JUSTIFIED?

You may be feeling bitter about having to retire, or even about choosing to retire if things have turned out differently than you imagined. To evaluate fairly whether or not retirement is justified, you must review the period through which you have come and see how major events have formed the opinions by which you live.

The world was very different when you were young. There was very little security, the "work ethic" was unquestioned, and pensions and retirement were not expected. You probably didn't think about voluntary retirement and it was sprung on you too late in your life to permit your ready acceptance of it. You probably expected to work until old age forced a stop, well past 65.

Many feel that retirement is a direct statement that they are too old to be of further use, not just in the job but in anything. They believe they no longer have a valid reason to continue. That might be so if the sole purpose of life is to put in a full day at the same employment until forced to halt. But who decreed that? Until recently, even in the western world, the supply of the necessities of life was limited, and it was not possible in any country to do anything else but wring the last ounce of work out of everyone. Retirement could not be universal.

The advent of the automobile, truck, and tractor and the mechanical, chemical, and computer revolutions made possible increased production, so that since the turn of the century, hours of work have been greatly reduced. The reduction from the 72-hour work week to the 40-hour work week was a step forward in the improving quality of life. Retirement is another improvement — a gift made possible by the inventive genius of humans.

c. FINANCIAL SECURITY

Your income is probably more secure now than it was during your working life. You could have been fired, become ill or injured, necessitating either employment at a lower income or, perhaps, even unemployment with limited income from a disability pension. Your particular skill might have been eliminated by progress.

Continued employment depended on many things, but your retirement income is secure with no strings attached. Your government pensions are certain and indexed against inflation. Indeed, almost any contractual pension is also safe. There are many sources of aid open to you, and any retired person having financial problems should start by inquiring at the local municipal level. If the problem is beyond their power, you will be directed to the proper source.

d. THE IMPORTANCE OF INTERESTS AND ACTIVITIES

It is common for those who enter retirement unprepared to fail to see the necessity of keeping busy with satisfying pursuits. Activity can make life worthwhile, especially if you sincerely enjoy it.

The passage of time is a great healer and by keeping yourself occupied with satisfying interests, eventually most worries will fade away.

It is quite possible that, in addition to finding satisfying activities to fill your mind, you will find some that will replace the things you enjoyed most in your work. It is essential to understand yourself and your needs and then to find the ways to satisfy both.

e. ATTITUDE

Your attitude will play a most important part in determining if you will have a happy retirement. It is a controlling factor in morale, and high morale is sought by every competitor, organization, business, or team. It is recognized as an essential ingredient in becoming a winner in any field, and it contributes heavily to satisfaction and happiness.

High morale is based on the confidence that you can and will succeed. It can provide the strength to enable you to reach out and try new and often difficult things, or to put up with an inconvenience to enjoy something that you might otherwise pass by. It can impart an enthusiasm for life.

f. RELIGION

There is another very important factor that may affect your serenity or peace of mind. I know of no culture ever discovered, regardless of how isolated its location, that did not have strong beliefs in some system of gods or a superior power that controlled the world and those who live in it. For centuries, a strong religious faith has provided peace of mind for many and those who possess this treasure are fortunate to have the solace it brings.

In recent years, the discoveries of science have weakened the tenets of religions and have undermined their acceptance by many. People who have experienced this are left in a vacuum that is waiting to be filled. While this situation is not caused by retirement, as you grow older it is common to question the purpose of your life and whether or not there is a "hereafter." Unanswered questions may become stumbling blocks to your peace of mind.

After retirement, many who have drifted away find comfort in returning to their religious roots.

g. THE PROMISED SOLUTIONS

At the beginning of this chapter, solutions were promised. They are clear and simple:

(a) Identify and understand your problems.

(b) Put them in proper perspective.

(c) Take any necessary action to solve them.

(d) Find activities that will satisfy your personal requirements.

(e) Set up new goals with your spouse to provide a purpose for your lives and a direction for your energy. The satisfaction derived from their pursuit and achievement can make an important contribution to your happiness and peace of mind.

Retirement is, for many, one of the happiest stages of life. Some even take it early so they can start enjoying the life they always wanted. It can be that way for you, too, but only if you make it so.

4
CHOOSE FROM A SMORGASBORD OF ACTIVITIES

The morning you step out into the new world of retirement is like starting down the line at a smorgasbord with an empty plate. There is an appealing variety of dishes — some will please you, some will not. You are free to take your pick, fill your plate, and then come back for more. If you try something new, but do not enjoy it, you are not forced to eat it. There will be more than you can possibly sample, and there will not be room for everything.

Any activities that you enjoy now can be the base on which to build a plan for your retirement. You may have hobbies and activities you want to continue to pursue. The problem is that they probably won't fill this great new expanse of time. You can take extra training to improve your skill or knowledge and broaden your scope, but this may still not be sufficient.

If you find yourself with time on your hands, there is a wide choice of activities available. You must select those that appeal to you and then take the initiative to enjoy them. Even if you are restricted by cost or physical disability, there is still plenty to choose from. It is amazing how content many people with severe handicaps often are; most of them adjust to their disabilities and build happy lives. Although they must miss many activities, they find satisfactory alternatives.

If you are forced into unwanted retirement and feel that nothing can take the place of your job, change that thinking now. Once into these enjoyable activities, you will, like so many others, wish that you could have retired earlier! People who are bored have only themselves to blame for refusing to try new things. For your own sake as well as for those around you, be a sport and try!

In this chapter, there is a broad range of activities described to suit any kind of person: those who are active or inactive, those who are happiest in a group, or those who are loners.

Make up a mix that will provide the most satisfaction and that will cover all seasons. It is best to include some with obligations to a schedule to get you out of the house. Be sure to have a variety in order to avoid boredom.

a. SOCIAL ACTIVITIES

You may need to find new friends and social activities to take the place of those associated with employment. There are many opportunities, but you must find them and make the effort to participate. Many groups such as religious and municipal organizations stage seniors' events, often for a specific purpose such as exercise groups, dinners, or card games.

Card games are perhaps the most widely enjoyed seniors' social activity, as almost everyone plays. Being able to play opens up a whole new area, for card players are always seeking others to participate. Playing cards may bring more invitations to join others than any other contact. If you do not play, you will miss much of the social scene; have a friend teach you or take lessons.

Card-playing has another desirable feature, for if you are on vacation and staying in a hotel or trailer, you need only invite someone to play and, suddenly, other vacationers who were previously strangers become friends.

Sharing a meal with friends either at home or in a restaurant is an enjoyable social event. For many, it is their only social activity.

b. JOIN THE CLUB

A helpful move is to join a senior citizens' club. Established groups are located in almost every place of worship, regardless of the denomination. These are usually service groups organized to benefit anyone who wants to join; you don't have to be a member of the particular religious group to participate. As well, the YMCA, YWCA, YMHA, some municipalities, and other interested organizations also sponsor seniors' groups.

If there are several clubs available near your home, talk to some of the members of each before joining. You would be well advised to spend some time at each to ensure you choose the one with the most compatible membership and activities you enjoy. If there is no group near you, get together with a few others and start your own.

The American Association of Retired Persons (AARP) is an organization in which membership has much to offer those in or approaching retirement. It has a permanent head office staff that constantly monitors issues affecting the retired. There is a modest annual membership fee for which there are many advantages. Members receive the magazine *Modern Maturity*, which contains much of interest and value. There is also an AARP non-profit pharmacy service that provides reasonable prices and postage-paid home delivery, and there are special arrangements for auto and homeowners' insurance. Also offered are other money-saving advantages such as discounts granted by hotels and motels. You will be invited to join one of the 3,500 local chapters that could be a source of friends and interesting activities. For more information, contact the association at:

>American Association of Retired Persons
>1909 K Street N.W.
>Washington, D.C. 20049

c. PHYSICAL FITNESS

There is a widespread acceptance of the value of physical fitness for bodily and mental health. Those who do participate not only often find it a most enjoyable, beneficial, and absorbing activity, but claim that they look and feel better. As a bonus, it may make possible participation in more physically demanding activities, often to a greater age. Make sure you have a medical examination to determine your body's safe limits.

To be effective, a regular program is needed which can be chosen from many options, depending on what you enjoy and how much effort you wish to put into it. Walking and swimming can be the least demanding, but the effort can be increased if desired.

Regular periods of calisthenics, those exercises which you may have learned at school or in the services, may suffice. These may be supplemented with simple equipment such as weights or spring-loaded devices requiring greater exertion. Workout rooms with more sophisticated equipment are often available at community centers, public and private clubs, apartment complexes, and retirement communities.

Sports are part of maintaining physical fitness and participating has additional advantages. It helps give the feeling of being part of the active world, makes you feel younger, and gets you out of the home and in contact with others, which are all things of importance at this stage.

A useful book regarding health and physical fitness is *Fit After Fifty*, another title in the Self-Counsel Retirement Series.

d. SPORTS

There are many sports suitable for older people; some are enjoyed by men and women in their eighties. Some sports are for the individual, others require a team. Some are strenuous, others are not.

When building your list, make a point of finding a variety of things to do in all seasons, such as curling in winter and tennis in summer. In the northern states, many outdoor sports are seasonal, but there may be indoor versions of them or other indoor games available through the winter which makes it possible to make up an assortment of activities.

1. Tennis

People are retiring at an earlier age while physically active, and more of them are playing tennis. It is a year-round outdoor game where weather permits, and in the northern states where outdoor tennis is seasonal, indoor courts are becoming widely available. While competitive tennis is strenuous, older persons play at a level within their strength. Many municipalities have public courts, and most retirement communities have private clubs. Playing tennis can provide the benefits of exercise, enjoyment, and can introduce you to a group of your peers.

2. Curling

Curling is an international sport of the colder countries and is widely played in the northern states. After retirement, you are likely to find most team sports too strenuous for your participation, but curling is a notable exception. It is the ideal sport for retired men and women. It need not be expensive and can be practiced either by team members in a competitive schedule or by occasional players participating as desired.

Young people work hard at the sweeping part of the game, but older groups generally leave it for the individual to decide how hard he or she wants to work. Many people curl into their eighties and even some with physical disabilities are able to participate. There is no real work in throwing the stone; it is simply raised from the ice, swung slowly as a pendulum, and released to allow its weight to carry it along on the smooth ice.

Everyone is welcome. There is a place on each team for the inexperienced player as the "lead." Leads are often in short supply and the more experienced players expect and welcome them.

The real aim of the game at this stage of life is social, so there is no pressure to win as there is in younger leagues. There are times available for men's and women's games as well as mixed games in which you can participate with your spouse. Start at any age; someone will be glad to teach you.

An added bonus is the number of people you will meet. There are eight people in every game and you will meet other teams as well as you play through a season.

To the newcomer, the courtesy shown to all in curling and the desire to make the game a pleasant experience is very noticeable. Curling is a game with no referees and no one is expected to "make" every shot. Everyone is welcome except a complainer.

Do not hesitate to try curling. You will probably have friends who play, or you can look up the local arenas and ask for information. There is almost certainly a nearby group that will welcome you.

3. Golf

Golf is played widely in all regions, although it is seasonal in colder areas. It is also a game that spouses often enjoy together. There are courses of all kinds, varying in degrees of physical effort required, expense, and skill.

One of the recent developments is the "executive" or "par-three" course. These courses are much shorter with holes running about half the length of those on a regular course. They are generally less challenging, and they fill the need for those who lack the skill and stamina to handle 18 full-length holes. They are made to order for the non-expert retired couple.

Power carts can be rented at most courses; they can help reduce the physical effort required. Choose the course that best suits you.

Another advantage of taking up golf is that it is available everywhere you go. It can be a real interest on a southern winter holiday. You can learn at any age. If you regard it as a pleasant outdoor experience, rather than a challenge to become an expert, you can learn to play well enough. Courses are not crowded in the off hours during weekdays and you will be welcome as a learner at that time. Join a club or "pay as you play." It need not be expensive.

4. Swimming

Swimming in the ocean, in lakes, or in swimming pools is one of the most enjoyable experiences of childhood. As an adult, your obligations may have left you little time for swimming, but now these obligations have gone. It is still as much fun as ever, and in addition, it offers many health benefits. Swimming is a complete exercise; you use every muscle. Also, swimming can have a therapeutic effect because it takes your mind off other things.

There may be suitable local waters but pools are the main source for retired people. There are indoor public and private pools which are open year round, and almost every retirement facility has one. If you don't know how to swim, don't let that get in your way; you can still learn. Many pools have staff who give lessons to adults. Many also have exercise programs that take place in the water. The buoyancy of the water can assist those with muscular problems to exercise.

5. Hunting

Hunting is an American tradition, and many people have hunted all their lives. More women are participating in hunting, and equipment manufacturers are producing suitable items for them.

There are usually open seasons and bag limits to be observed, and sporting goods stores usually carry brochures listing the rules. You might want to join an association of anglers and hunters, go to the meetings, and meet new friends. Or, join a gun club; most groups need new members from time to time and you don't need to be an expert shot. Don't hesitate to participate.

Across the country, there is a broad range of hunting opportunities offered from small birds to big game. Migrating waterfowl are available almost everywhere in the autumn; doves can be hunted in the mid and southern states in fall and winter; and quail hunting is popular almost everywhere. Every area has its local favorites, and in the off-season there are usually some non-regulated species available.

6. Fishing

Fishing has always fascinated both men and women as it contains elements of gambling, surprise, and mystery. It is, after all, one of the rare sources of a free lunch. To many, "the catch" is the goal, but even more important is the opportunity it affords to enjoy the peace, quiet, and beauty of the outdoors.

Anglers' clubs or associations exist in most areas. Fees are minimal and joining one may be a good source of information and instruction if required.

Now that you have the time, you will be surprised to find how many places there are for reasonably good fishing, even in or near very crowded cities. Spend some time around the available water and ask questions at the marinas and tackle stores to learn about renting tackle and to get directions and advice. By starting this way, you will know better what to buy if you decide to continue with the sport.

Summer, with its better weather and open water, is the usual season for fishing, but it is a sport that may be enjoyed all year even in the colder areas. Ice fishing is very popular now that improved facilities are available. Snowmobiles and tracked vehicles have made safe transportation to more distant spots a routine operation. You need not have your own vehicle as transportation is often provided to the rental fish huts.

7. Boating

Boating is possible almost anywhere there is water. If you don't own a boat, start by renting and see if your interest develops. It is best to have some experienced person accompany you in the beginning as there are many possible hazards with which the uninitiated may not be familiar.

There are many types of boats ranging from skiffs, punts, and canoes for those who wish to propel themselves, to power boats with small outboard motors, to yachts. Sailing has a fascination of its own and there is usually at least one sailing club on any water large enough to support it.

Many people find that boating opens a new world of interest for them. A craft with living accommodation may take the place of a cottage, or in warmer climes may provide a winter vacation.

The Power Squadron and the U.S. Coast Guard auxiliaries offer excellent courses on boating and safety. As the waters become more crowded, you would do well to take one of these courses to ensure a safe and enjoyable hobby.

8. Walking and hiking

Don't neglect walking as a combined form of sport, physical activity, and an interesting way to pass the time. Walking is an activity that your doctor will probably recommend, but to be of value, it should be done at a suitable rate and for a long enough distance.

If you tire of walking the same routes, try some variety. Go to new parts of the city or country. Most people who have lived in an area have not seen its points of interest, the ones that the sightseeing tours visit. Why not plan your walks to lead you through accessible districts of possible interest? You may be surprised to discover new and fascinating haunts.

Clubs and other organizations often plan walks to interest people in wildlife or bird watching. These walks are usually advertised to the public. Why not go at least once to see if you enjoy it?

9. Bowling

Indoor bowling is popular with both men and women and is a combination of sport, exercise, and a social event. It is most actively pursued by clubs formed by work groups, churches, senior citizens' organizations, or other associations. Teams are formed and they play and compete on a regular schedule.

Don't neglect an opportunity to participate for it can be a fine interest all year round. Most bowling alleys have reserved times for leagues as well as open times when the general public can play. This provides an opportunity to go on a prearranged outing or on the spur of the moment as a couple, a family, or with a group of friends.

10. Shuffleboard

Shuffleboard is one of the most common games of retired people. It is played on a smooth concrete court down which the player uses a long-handled cue to shoot a disk toward a marked goal at the end. Little physical effort is required and it can be played by singles or teams. Almost every resort, motel, and retirement community has courts.

e. ENTERTAINMENT

Entertainment will have a new place in your life now that you have much more time and the freedom to spend it in this very enjoyable way. You are free to choose the time when the entertainment is most readily available and the prices are lowest. For example, many organizations have special discounts for seniors but they are restricted to certain times of the day or week. Don't hesitate to ask if special rates are available wherever you go.

Some theater chains issue special identifying cards that you must show to purchase the ticket at a discount. Inquire at your local theater for more information. They will tell you what proof of age is required and give you your identification application. You can usually get even larger discounts if you attend a function as a member with an organization or group. A chartered bus, for example, may reduce the transportation cost and add to the fun.

Look into the available opportunities. Read the advertisements and, above all, ask your other retired friends. Most of them take great pride in being a source of information and are very pleased to be asked for it.

f. HOBBIES

There are many hobbies that are of absorbing interest and that continually demand that you expand in skill, knowledge, and technology. You might want to pursue your hobby for personal pleasure only or work at it seriously with a definite goal in mind — perhaps to meet acceptable commercial standards and sell your product.

Most boards of education, colleges, and technical schools offer inexpensive classes that may fill your needs. Private lessons will cost more, but may be necessary if you want to develop a really professional finish. In some areas there are privately run trade schools that aim to develop a commercial standard of skill in a trade in which employment is available.

It may be an advantage to strive for saleable results from your hobby. You will have a goal and be forced to improve, practice, and keep at it. This will assist in overcoming the lethargy and loss of interest that can so easily come to the retired person who is no longer subject to the demands and discipline of a job. Selling your work can also give that sense of achievement and success that may otherwise be lacking in your life.

Some hobbies, such as those described below, have almost unending possibilities and are usually accompanied by membership in a very active club or group that can provide opportunities for an expanding circle of friends and social activities.

1. Woodworking

You might try your hand at building furniture, boats, cupboards, or an addition to your cabin. Some people enjoy making models or furniture from kits, others from more complex plans requiring considerable skill. If you have no experience and you need training, look into courses at your local community or technical school. Once you learn how to measure, cut, join, smooth, and nail, you have the rudiments to do almost anything. Your early efforts may be rough, but with practice and a serious interest, you can become proficient.

Most libraries have many books showing the structural methods used in making anything from a doghouse to a violin. You can also learn about furniture refinishing and other carpentry techniques.

2. Gardening

If you think of gardening as simply planting, watering, weeding, and watching things grow, think again. That is only the beginning to what can be an exciting hobby. If you are interested, you can read up on those plants that interest you and become an expert. You may then go on to plant breeding and even the development of new strains. The hobby opens the way to flower shows, clubs, and new friends with similar interests.

You don't even need a big space; apartment balcony gardens are common. In some locations, you can rent small garden plots, and, if you grow vegetables, you can help deflect rising food costs.

Gardening need not stop with the end of summer. Indoor gardening under lights can let you enjoy your hobby year round. A greenhouse can be relatively inexpensive, but even that is not necessary. Fluorescent lights permit the establishment of a garden in the basement at practically no cost. You may grow winter blooms or have your plants started indoors and ready to transplant when spring arrives.

In the south, where growth is continual, there may be specific times to plant each species so a series of plants and vegetables can be chosen to make it a year-round outdoor activity.

3. Photography

Everyone enjoys looking at pictures. Taking a good photograph requires skill as well as luck, and it involves an understanding of composition, lighting, and timing.

This hobby can be pursued with an inexpensive camera or can be expanded as far as your interest desires and your finances permit. Camera clubs are everywhere. Their members will welcome you and be most willing to teach you new techniques. You might find you even move on to developing your own negatives, and printing your own pictures.

4. Bird watching

As well as finding and observing birds, it can be fascinating to study identifying marks, record normal seasonal migration dates, and look for unusual species.

This interest, again, can lead to new friends through shared interest and club membership. Local clubs often gather annual migration records and public participation is invited in seasonal "watches."

A bird feeder in your garden can keep you busy observing all year. You should also buy a good bird book and a pair of binoculars to assist you in identifying new species.

g. CONTINUING EDUCATION

If you have thought of continuing your education, now is the time. In recent years there has been a broadening of opportunities, range of programs offered, and entrance requirements.

There are basically two classifications. The first is the study of academic subjects. You can attend classes simply for your pleasure, or to attain high school or university graduation status. You can often do this through a local institution or by correspondence. University degrees, in particular, have become more readily available in this way.

The second classification includes those subjects that lead to the development of skills. A growing number of institutions offer courses in subjects such as art, house repairs, gourmet cooking, and acting. They also teach a large number of commercial subjects.

If you want part-time employment, you may find that a course will either provide new skills for you or bring rusty ones up to saleable standards. You may take such a course in the evening while you are still working in order to be ready for retirement, or it may be best for you to take it as a full-time activity after you have stopped working.

You might also want to look into part-time employment in the field of continuing education. Many school boards now employ retired persons as part-time teachers for instructing children, tutoring those requiring extra attention, and conducting language classes for newcomers. Formal teaching qualifications are not usually required. If interested, inquire at your local board.

You can also combine an interest in studies with an interest in travel by joining the Elderhostel organization. This organization offers opportunities for short-term courses at institutions all over the world. Participants must be 60 or older. Spouses who are over 50 may accompany a participant. For more information, contact:

>Elderhostel
>80 Boylston Street
>Suite 400,
>Boston, Massachusetts 02116

h. LIBRARIES AND READING

You may find a hobby that has no cost. A fine example of this is reading, perhaps the most widely pursued interest of the retired. It can be expensive if you buy all the books and magazines you would like to read, but a good alternative is using the public library. It is full of interesting reading, instructive titles, and current magazines. You can read them there or take them home.

If you walk into a library with no object in mind and simply look around and read titles, you will almost certainly find yourself taking down one or more books or magazines and becoming interested. It will be surprising if it doesn't result in your taking books home and you may find yourself starting to read much more, or having a new interest in a hobby you read about but had never considered before. If you don't use a library regularly, visit one and let nature take its course!

i. POLITICS

Everyone should be interested in politics and government; they are the basis of democracy. At federal, state, and municipal levels, there are associations that remain active between elections. Most locally elected people also have a support organization where much of the work is done by volunteers.

Choose a candidate, a party, or an issue you wish to support and turn up at the meeting. Join the organization and offer to help. You will be welcome; this is just what is needed and can develop into a real interest for you.

At election time, there is often paid work within the association or at polling booths. Such jobs, of course, go to the faithful who were there ahead of time. Don't ignore this activity if you have an interest in the government at any level. You can also help keep the views and needs of retired people before the politicians. Retired people are a steadily increasing percentage of the population. This is a very important voting block and receives attention from all levels of government. However, requests made by organizations that represent a number of people carry more weight with a politician than requests made by individuals. There are organizations, such as AARP, that promote the views of seniors and aim for government support. Your participation is needed and will be welcome, so consider joining any such organization available in your district that advances ideas you consider desirable.

j. CREATIVE ACTIVITIES

Some people are creative by nature and must use their gift to feel fulfilled. If you have a special creative interest, seek out a group of like-minded people. Some groups form to help each other; others are led by an instructor. Many school boards have night school classes that can lead to more serious study involving private lessons.

Once you become involved in art, you discover a whole new world. You see things so much more clearly and appreciate the real beauty. An art gallery takes on a new interest and a quick trip through one is no longer enough. You can spend a whole day studying one painting! Local exhibitions become an event to watch for.

If you are creative, try different things until you find the application that interests you. It may be clay modelling, painting, carving, or whatever; any interest becomes fascinating and engrossing once you get into it.

Most people feel that they must have inborn talent to do creative work, but this is not so. It has been said that 90% of painting is learned and only 10% is natural talent. This means that almost anyone who is interested in and enjoys this creative hobby can learn to paint well enough to achieve satisfying results. Instruction and then practice are the basic requirements.

If you are going to enjoy painting, practice will be most interesting as you see your skill improve with each picture. If you are interested, don't be afraid to try.

k. TRAVEL

1. Take advantage of discounts

If you want to travel in your retirement, take advantage of special rates available to seniors. Most are advertised, but many are given only on request. Usually you must ask to find them, so never fail to do so when registering or buying a ticket. There are often special lower cost tours geared to seniors; they are paced more slowly and provide for any special needs.

Wherever you wish to go — to the local museum, Florida, or to see the Great Buddha in Thailand — you should be able to find "package tours." These have many advantages, more so now that you are older and can use the extra help. The cost is usually fixed and your baggage, hotels, transportation and, sometimes, meals are all looked after for you. You will probably find compatible companions in the group and there is always someone responsible if you need assistance, making it more comfortable for a single person to travel.

Ask air, bus, and rail lines about fares, package plans, etc. Travel agents often have specials; look around, it is surprising what is available. Don't give up because you think the expense will be too great; there are many low-cost package tours, charter flights, and group plans. You may be pleasantly surprised that you can afford many memorable trips. Some are now planned specifically for seniors.

2. The trailer and the recreational vehicle

There are two different kinds of equipment: the trailer and the recreational vehicle (RV).

The trailer is towed behind a car or light truck. It ranges from a simple, ingeniously designed box on two wheels which opens up to provide the platform for a tent, to a much larger, more luxurious vehicle.

The RV is a self-propelled, bus-like vehicle with its own motor. Both the larger trailers and the RVs are equipped with toilets, kitchens, sinks, stoves, refrigerators, and beds. They are in reality, small, mobile apartments. Most people find the facilities for living quite adequate and easy to use and maintain. They are compact homes that accompany you to provide a familiar, inexpensive dwelling, and you avoid the inconvenience of packing and unpacking. They also provide the camaraderie of trailer park life, where it is usually easier to make friends than in motels or hotels.

Living in this manner introduces you to a new way of life. Sometimes it is the only home, but more often it becomes the traveling home that is used to go south in the winter, north in the summer, and often anywhere else you fancy in between. Stay in one place as long as you wish, move when you desire. There are trailer camps almost everywhere, some in public parks, others privately operated. Most have sewage, power, and water hookups. Central buildings often provide supplies and recreational, laundry, and shower facilities. People who enjoy this type of life are inclined to be friendly and quickly make contact with each day's new neighbors. Those who enjoy each other's company often form groups that travel together or that meet at prearranged destinations.

For many, retirement brings the opportunity to indulge in this kind of life for the first time. It has numerous advantages, the most important of which is the way in which it can lift you out of a rut and provide a new and exciting lifestyle. The contact with different people and the opportunity to try new things and see different areas can stimulate and revitalize your life and outlook. Many people have found it to be the means of building a fascinating life in retirement.

If the lifestyle appeals to you, it is a simple thing to investigate. Go to nearby trailer camps; the people there will be happy to talk to you. Visit dealers to see the different types. At first, you would be wise to rent different units for short trips so you can find out if you do enjoy this lifestyle and, if so, exactly what features you prefer when you decide to purchase a unit.

For more information, see *Mobile Retirement Handbook*, another title in the Self-Counsel Retirement Series.

l. VOLUNTEER WORK

Shakespeare once wrote, "Mercy...is twice blest, it blesseth him that gives and him that takes." (*Merchant of Venice*, Act IV, Scene 1)

The same can be said of volunteer work. There is a tremendous need for people willing to give assistance to the disadvantaged. If you have time to give and a desire to help, there is plenty of scope. It would be impossible to list all the things that are done by volunteers, but the range is broad.

If you derive personal satisfaction from serving others, now is the time to reach out and grasp the opportunity. Your help is needed but you need to consider your own personality before you volunteer. Some people find it too difficult to work with people who have certain disabilities or who live in difficult situations. But the choice of activities is so broad that you should be able to find something suitable.

If you don't know where to begin, ask any religious leader for suggestions. Try the YMCA, the Community

Chest office, or the Red Cross. Many cities have a volunteer center to advise those wishing to do volunteer work of available opportunities, so inquire and locate an opportunity suitable for you. The variety of opportunities is great and changes with the area. Volunteers are needed to work in the following fields:

With children — social services, teaching, tutoring, leisure time activities, and day care

With the elderly and handicapped — visiting, delivering meals, craft work, shopping, telephoning

Service to immigrants — information, teaching, social outreach

Hospitals — visiting, crafts, shopping escort

Mental health — distress centers, telephone counseling, crafts, group involvement

Corrections — a friend to one on probation or parole

m. FOR SELF-STARTERS AND LEADERS

It has been estimated that about 10% of the population are leaders and the rest are followers. During working years, economic necessity and the urgings of parents and spouse force even the most shy person out to work. When that phase is over, many followers are inclined to remain at home rather than start out to build their new lives, and it is they who frequently give up, have difficulty in adjusting, or simply fade away.

They need help to become interested in life again. They can be encouraged with a push or an invitation from family or friends to get out and join in some activity. Those who are leaders and self-starters can fulfill their own ambitions by starting something new and inviting others to join them.

5
PERSONAL AND FAMILY RELATIONSHIPS IN RETIREMENT

In many ways, married and single people will have the same problems and opportunities after retirement and should, therefore, take the same steps to prepare for it. There are, however, some basic differences that require separate consideration.

Those who are married will have the support of a spouse to fall back on, but will also have new problems injected into their relationship. This will require mutual effort and understanding to avoid friction.

For single people, the replacement of job-related personal relationships may be one of their greatest priorities. To better understand both groups we shall look at the situation from the standpoint of married and single people separately and the contribution that family and friends can make to their lives after retirement.

Whether you are married or living alone, your relationships with those who care about you become more important. Loneliness is one of the most serious problems of older people. Love and friendship prevent or cure loneliness, and the assistance of others, if not a necessity, can be a comfort.

a. REPLACE EMPLOYMENT CONTACTS

In chapter 2, the value of the contacts made with your fellow workers was discussed. In retirement all this is lost, for the break with your fellow employees is usually complete. You will find yourself forced out of their circle and kept out by the walls within which they work. It is difficult to maintain their friendships, and, even if you do, they cannot fill your new needs during the working day when you want friends to help use this new-found time. Their spare time may be used for chores and family matters, and they may have little time for you. You will be alone in a strange and unknown world. It may be a very startling shock and the contribution that these people made must be replaced for the sake of your health and happiness.

In addition to replacing these personal contacts, another need arises. As the years go by, your physical condition and strength deteriorate and the assistance of others in the simple matters of daily living may become of great importance. At some point, you may be able to continue in your own home only with help; without it, it may be necessary to enter an institution where help is available.

Expanding relationships to provide love, friendship, and support becomes one of the basic needs in these years. Knowing you are accepted by others and have friends is important to your self-esteem. Once your job is gone, you need people to keep you in contact with the world outside yourself and to help you avoid becoming too dependent on your spouse or family.

b. THE STRAINS OF RETIREMENT ON MARRIAGE

There are major changes in retirement, which, if not amicably solved, can cause a breakdown in your relationship and perhaps in your marriage. This is unfortunate, for retirement is a time when husband and wife will be spending more time together and will be increasingly dependent on each other for companionship and assistance.

There will be change, but the important thing is to use the change well and understand what is happening. Use it as an opportunity to make this a new and enjoyable stage in your partnership.

Before retirement, you both had separate days and you enjoyed evenings together. There were things to tell each other and the variety of contributions brought from your separate days made your time together enjoyable.

Think of the change! Being together all the time can be boring. You experience the same things. There is nothing new to discuss. Both may have lost outside interests. Such a situation may spoil the most valuable thing any married person can have at this time: a happy spouse and a happy home.

No one would knowingly cause this kind of problem. There is no need to, provided you make the effort to avoid them.

1. A wife's independent life

Women who have been employed have had working lives that brought the same benefits and problems as their husband's jobs. On retirement, they may suffer the same losses. On the other hand, women usually retire at an earlier age and are often established at home, with independent interests, when their husbands retire.

Women who have remained at home to raise a family, have seen their children grow up and move out, and have then been free to plan their own time. They have made independent and enjoyable lives of their own. They may have chosen hobbies, volunteer, social and/or recreational activities, and time spent with friends. They may have chosen to work full- or part-time. Whatever activities they chose did not involve their husbands. These personal and separate lives were a definite part of their identities, as important to them as jobs were to their husbands.

The life of a homemaker is much more than housekeeping and shopping. They may continue with these tasks after their spouses retire — in this respect homemakers never retire, but it is a mistake to assume that this is their only life. Men sometimes think that retirement will give them the chance to be around home to keep their wives company. They assume their presence will not change things and will perhaps make the days more interesting. This may not be the way the women see it.

2. Who will be in charge?

Housework and shopping may be a source of friction. After one or both of you retire, the division of labor will change. The problem is that each of you may have very different ideas of how things should be done, and both of you may attempt to assert your standards and methods and try to take over as the boss.

You need to sit down and redefine your roles. If one of you has been responsible for most of the housework in the past, then the other should ask where the most help can be given. You might want to list the tasks and assign duties.

3. Don't spoil it!

Studies reveal that retiring men often find it more difficult to adjust than women. Women may be more adaptable, have a greater interest in their homes, and have more social activities than their husbands. Unless the man is able to develop independent interests, he may be frightened and concerned about the future. He needs someone to help him and the obvious person is his spouse, the only one who has any deep personal interest in him. He may find himself following her around the house, expecting constant attention. If you fall into this trap, you are reducing your spouse to the position of a personal servant.

This is a most unfair and one-sided attitude. It is not a solution, for not only does it provide nothing of interest for either spouse, but it may spoil the relationship, making both unhappy and resentful.

Many wives who have stayed at home feel that the husband has worked all his life, often under considerable pressure, and now this is his time. She does not understand what he needs or can do, and therefore hesitates to interfere, and tries to help by staying at home with him. This is neither a fair nor effective solution. It is up to both to take the initiative and find activities and interests of their own.

Discuss the future and work out a mutually acceptable plan. Accept each other as equal partners. While working, the demands of the job were paramount, but this is no longer true. Now is your opportunity to do those things together that you have wanted to do but that were not previously possible. At the same time, you may both keep many of your independent interests. To achieve this, decide what you wish to do together, what is most important to each one individually, and work out a schedule to allocate the time to make them fit together.

4. Both can benefit

The best decisions are usually made in an atmosphere of trust and goodwill; the worst when one of the participants feels that the other wants to dominate and get an unfair share. Selfishness in the demands made by either person without considering the wishes of the other could cause feelings of animosity or of "being used," making a mutually satisfactory solution impossible. By granting your spouse's most important wishes and showing a willingness to compromise, you set a conciliatory tone and may receive the same treatment in return.

Professionals who help couples with marital problems often state that the solutions are frequently found in improving attitudes. They refer to the way in which courting couples act. Each person emphasizes his or her good qualities and suppresses those that may not please. They are courteous and considerate; selfishness is restrained. The whole relationship is directed toward harmony and mutual enjoyment of the time together.

This behavior is easier under the spell of new love and romance. After many years of marriage, courtesy and consideration may be forgotten. Professionals suggest that it is possible to reintroduce romance into a mature marriage, and this can inject a spark of real pleasure and interest into your life. Try it. In this atmosphere, it is likely that a solution bringing the greatest benefit to both parties can be achieved.

Full personal development arising from respect for each other's individuality and desires, coupled with the benefits and close companionship of marriage, can do much to achieve the second requirement for happiness — to love and be loved.

c. YOUR FAMILY

The main source of friendship and/or love and support comes from your family. It is a rare person who does not have some relatives. The more distant relationships that might be ignored by those who have a large family and children of their own can be of utmost importance to those who have not. Even those now single may have children from a previous marriage. Whatever your position, cherish your relatives and strengthen the connections.

The family is constantly changing as new members enter by birth or marriage, and as those within it grow through the successive stages of life. A three-generation family may be a self-contained and self-regenerating unit. There are children to enjoy, mature people to help them, and younger adults to assist older members. As you grow older many of these changes benefit you.

The importance of the family relationship may not be entirely recognized prior to retirement because it has not yet fully developed. Your own life may not have arrived at the point where the need is apparent or the contribution you can make is appreciated. Its importance is obvious if you discuss it with and observe those living in retirement. Grandchildren and family are the most important topic of conversation. Many who move away from them to fill other interests soon find that nothing takes their place and often move back to be near them. You may be appreciated as a sitter, to look after the children, to give parents time for other things. Do not avoid this, for it is one of the connections that binds a family together.

d. FAMILY RELATIONSHIPS

In the past, three or more generations of a family frequently lived together. Under the circumstances that then existed, particularly on farms, it could work well. Everyone's help was needed, there was more living space, the hours of work were longer, there was less leisure time in which friction could occur, and parents were accorded greater respect. This situation may still exist in rural settings. There are also some cultures that place greater importance on family solidarity than others. Where family relationships are pleasant, flexible, and everyone loves and enjoys each other, living together can be a fine arrangement. More often, however, it is not a happy situation, and it is preferable to have the generations living separately but in contact.

e. YOU BECOME THE RECEIVER

The stage of your life in which you constantly gave has turned into another where you may become the receiver. If you have children, they are by now probably on their own. That period in which their actions may have placed a strain on your relations and thrown up barriers between you has ended. They could not learn from your experience but had to do so from their own. The crash landings and the burnt fingers from which you could not save them not only served to cut the apron strings, but also matured them and may have restored you to your rightful position as their most valuable friend and ally. No other relationship can be as trustworthy, loving, and secure.

As they become more firmly established financially, they no longer need your support. If they have a family of their own, they now recognize and appreciate what you have done for them. They were once dependent on you but the relationship reverses and as the years go on you may need and rely on their help.

f. GRANDCHILDREN

A new and most pleasing aspect enters with the arrival of grandchildren. Their full value cannot be explained, it must be experienced. It is a natural instinct to continue the race, and their presence assures it during your lifetime. They bring back your younger years. We all love children, but these are not ordinary children: they are your grandchildren. If you show interest they return it with unfeigned and enthusiastic love. Who would not respond and feel flattered when a child so obviously enjoys your company?

You will be wanted, for this is an opportunity to give as well as receive. You have a contribution to make to both children and grandchildren and they may learn much from you. The young ones will observe you going through the final stage of the life cycle and will pick up knowledge to use in preparation for their later years. You can teach them your values. More may be taken in and stored away for future use than is realized at the time. You are in an enviable position when compared to their parents, for not being responsible for discipline means you can concentrate on enjoying them. It makes a difference that often enables grandparents to maintain a hold on their grandchildren and to reach them when they are breaking away from and perhaps ignoring their parents.

g. SONS- OR DAUGHTERS-IN-LAW

The family expansion brings a possible problem, for the marriage of your child introduces a stranger into a key position. This new son- or daughter-in-law can decide to welcome or reject you, and that decision may be made in response to your treatment and how you accepted him or her as a spouse for your son or daughter or if you have attempted to interfere with their lives. It will obviously be an advantage to have a warm and friendly relationship with your in-law if you are to see and enjoy each other with any frequency.

Avoid complaining, for listening to it is no pleasure. Keep your proper place; raising their children is their responsibility, not yours. You had your turn. To interfere may make you most unwelcome. Visits will be more enjoyable and frequent if they are made for the pleasure they bring, rather than grudgingly as a duty that must be performed.

About one of three marriages now breaks down, which introduces a disruption at the family's heart. Feelings can run high, sides may be taken, and one group may have little to do with the other. If this situation exists, it may tear at your peace of mind. If any grandchildren are in the custody of the one with whom you are not on good terms, there may be difficulty in seeing them. Not only will you miss them, but they may be scarred by bitterness that can affect them the rest of their lives. These unfortunate side effects can be lessened if you are able to keep an open mind and remain on good terms with both partners. By so doing, the personal hurt to both you and your family will be lessened and the benefits you derive from the relationships, and those which you contribute, are more likely to continue.

h. FRIENDS, OLD AND NEW

The second main source of support comes from friends. There is a depth of comfort, feeling, and understanding between old friends that takes years to grow and it is desirable to turn to them first. The newly available time makes it possible to spend more of it with them and perhaps re-open connections that may have been interrupted by the demands of raising a family or earning a living. You are a fortunate person if there are enough friends to fill your needs.

If not, turn to other retired men and women, for they are in the same position and are looking for new friends too. The problem in the larger cities is to find and meet those who have interests similar to your own. To do so, you must go out and visit those places where they may be found.

6
THE SINGLE PERSON

As a single person, you have the same needs as someone who is married. You need enough secure income to live in an acceptable manner, to love and be loved, and to be satisfied with the way you spend your time.

About one-third of the population aged 65 to 70 is single. Over two-thirds of this group were once married but have lost their spouses through death or divorce. In the 70 and over age group, the proportion of singles rises to one-half, and this increases as the groups grow older. The majority of them have suffered one of the most severe shocks that can be experienced — the loss of their spouse — and their adjustment to retirement may be more difficult than for their married counterparts.

The basic difference between a married and single person at this time is that the single does not have the support of a spouse to provide a built-in companion and helpmate. The singles must find their new activities themselves. Friends may be sympathetic and try to include them in their activities, but singles just do not fit well. This loss of married friends and the kind of activities enjoyed by couples may be deeply felt.

All married couples have to face the fact that, at some point, death will take one spouse and leave the other alone. However, this is not the end of everything. It is quite possible to make a new, satisfying, and meaningful life with others who are in the same position.

a. THE OPPORTUNITIES

The opportunities for enjoyment and fulfillment for single people have broadened greatly in recent years. As the proportion of young people in the population shrinks, and the number of older people expands, businesses are placing greater emphasis on filling new demands. All levels of government, too, are trying to recognize and live up to their responsibilities. Retired people are asking for the things they want and are helping build the organizations to satisfy their needs.

The opportunities for single women have changed greatly. Until recently, many things were closed to women and they were welcome at others only when they were accompanied by a man. Now they can go anywhere alone; even those previously exclusively male clubs accept women as members.

All these things, however, are like attractions set up at an amusement park or fair: they are there for your enjoyment, but you must act to buy the ticket and enter.

1. Organized activities

One of your greatest priorities may be making new social connections and finding new friends. There are many organizations to help: senior citizens' centers, churches, and religious and ethnic organizations, all of which often provide a meeting place where retired people with similar needs and interests can come together to fulfill them. They usually have permanent quarters, open daily. There is always something going on. There may be card games, crafts, courses of interest to the members, lunches, organized trips, and dances. Everyone is welcome regardless of marital status or sex. It is one place where men and women, single or otherwise, may be together and may help fill the desire of single people to mix with the opposite sex. The permanent staff are often able to help with problems or can direct you to other more suitable sources. The members have a wealth of information about activities, discounts, and other useful facts.

The possibilities for fulfillment and happiness through friendship and activities with others are very broad, so a single person need not spend a secluded, dull, or lonely life. Once again, all this is out there waiting; what you get is up to you.

2. Financial concerns

The financial position of single retired people will vary widely. Those who have worked all their lives and never married could be in the best financial situation. At the other end of the scale, widows who never worked in paid employment are, as a group, in the worst financial position.

As retirement approaches, everyone, married or single, should take the same steps to understand what their financial situation will be and to make the best use of resources. Those who feel incapable of this task, perhaps because their now-departed spouse looked after this part of their affairs, should concentrate on learning how to do so, and/or seek the service of an accountant, trust company, or financial advisor. These financial matters are discussed in the next few chapters.

b. TO LOVE AND BE LOVED

People are individuals and needs vary widely. Some singles feel most comfortable in groups and draw strength and pleasure from numbers. Others must have privacy: to them, two is a crowd. They enjoy time alone and are not lonely. But even a loner requires love and support, and it becomes more essential as time goes on.

Most of us are somewhere in between. Your feelings in this matter will influence your relationship with family and friends, the home chosen, and the activities in which you participate. Determine what is best for you and make every effort to achieve it.

Love is a word with many shades of meaning. In blood relationships there is a difficult-to-define element that cannot be shared with others outside the family. It is real, you are born to it, and it cannot be surrendered. In marriage, love is the source of the deepest values.

There can be a deep affectionate attachment between friends that is also a form of love. More often this relationship is simply friendship, a less intense feeling of pleasure in each other's company, but nevertheless most satisfying. Friends may be called on to provide a much larger part of the requirements of love and friendship for single people and therefore assume a more important role in their lives.

By drawing on these sources (family and friends), a single person can build a network that will eliminate loneliness and provide the satisfactions of love and friendship.

c. SHOULD YOU MARRY?

Married couples come together for love, and they provide love and companionship for each other. Those who have not married by retirement age have probably remained single by choice and may elect to remain so. But those who were married previously often would prefer to marry again if they found a suitable spouse. There are many advantages. Marrying again can provide the love and companionship as well as financial benefits through the pooling of incomes.

The opportunity is there if you wish to pursue it. There are many potential partners with the same desire; there is someone who would be happy to have you — the trick is to find each other. You have been through this mill before and know the ropes. You succeeded once, you may do so again. Marriage is not only for the young; you have as much to offer to a spouse of your own age now as you had to offer another when you were younger. Once again it will be up to you to get out to see and be seen by potential partners.

d. LIVING ALONE

Living alone has disadvantages. Not only is there no built-in friend to ward off loneliness, but there is the loss of the pleasure of being with someone you enjoy.

There is little incentive to prepare an interesting meal, so you may tend to snack on easily prepared items, not maintain a proper diet and, as a consequence, your health may deteriorate. Those who do not maintain outside contacts may become very introverted and their mental powers may suffer. Alone, life can become a dull, uninteresting existence.

There are many advantages to living with a compatible person. A friend may be the key to your maintaining an interest in things other than yourself, to help in the daily tasks, and to assist in times of illness. Some people fear moving in with a friend because it may encroach on independence and there may be some loss of privacy. It may mean giving up valued possessions that have a cherished link with the past. Compromise on location or other features may be involved. These, however, may be relatively unimportant factors when compared with the advantages.

If you wish to live alone, there is a wide range of arrangements from which to choose, some of which may offer many of the advantages of living with a companion. Friends often take nearby apartments in the same building. Each maintains a private home, but the friends are nearby. They may see each other frequently, visiting is safe and easy, and they assist each other when required.

Group homes, residences that are rented or purchased by a group, are growing in number. Members may have individual rooms but share the common areas, work, and expenses. The final alternative is the retirement home in which meals are provided and housekeeping is done by the staff. Nursing care, entertainment, and hobbies and crafts are included. Residents may come and go as they please, but often group outings with transportation are provided. This is a possible solution for those who cannot continue to live alone and it does have much to offer when needed.

e. LIVING A SATISFACTORY LIFE

The third requirement for happiness is to feel that your life is being well lived, which comes down to a fruitful and satisfying use of time. Each of us has a mental list of things that we must do and standards that we must meet to feel satisfied and retain our personal respect.

These will vary from person to person, but it is important that you recognize yours and that provisions are made to satisfy them. Some may be obligations that may not yield pleasure or fun, but their performance may be essential to peace of mind. From then on you may need an assortment, some for mental and physical health, and others for enjoyment only. Only you can decide what will be needed to provide this satisfaction and peace of mind.

7
MONEY MATTERS

One of the basic requirements for happiness is having enough secure income for a satisfactory life. A life disturbed by financial worries is unlikely to be happy.

There will be many changes to your income at retirement. The money from your regular paycheck will be replaced by money from other sources. Many of your expenditures could be eliminated or reduced, and there are many possibilities of increasing your income. The only people who have no such opportunities are those whose entire incomes will be from fixed pensions, who have no money or significant saleable assets, and who cannot or do not wish to earn additional income.

The next six chapters will show what remains from pre-retirement sources, what new items there may be to add to it, and how your cost of living may change.

Because your sources of income may be entirely new, the amount perhaps greatly reduced, and the ways in which you spend it very different, it is essential that you make the effort to learn the facts in order to simplify your decision making.

For example, you may have to choose between two hobbies or activities because of the cost. Often it is possible to eliminate expense without sacrificing much pleasure and, by so doing, to bring your income and expenditures into line. By simply thinking objectively about your expenditures, you may find better ways to save money.

You may be busy and short of time now but once you retire, you will have time to burn and will be seeking useful and profitable ways to employ it. Planning your finances is one of the better ways.

If you dislike this type of work or if you don't think you are able to do it, get the assistance of an accountant. However, first, you must gather certain information about your income and expenses. Your records need not itemize every small detail, but should clearly list all sources of income on a family basis. All expenditures may be grouped in broad classifications that clearly reveal any problems.

a. CALCULATE YOUR TOTAL JOINT INCOME

Be careful not to oversimplify your joint income calculation. Most employed people have some payments made for them by the employer, such as medical insurance, pension plans, company car, etc. If you spend any of your capital or capital gains on living expenses, you should consider this as income.

Begin by listing any income that you or your spouse earn. All you need is paper, a pencil, and, unless you are a good accountant, an eraser or perhaps a calculator. Have some plain paper for doing your rough work and some sheets or a book ruled with horizontal lines and with two vertical columns for dollars and cents on the right of the page. These are available at most stationery stores and will help you organize your work and avoid mistakes.

It is best to calculate a full year's income and expenditures in order to catch all seasonal factors. If you use the last full year, you will also have income records from your employment (Form W-2) and an income tax return to use as a check.

First, list all items of income. (See the checklist in section **b.** following.) Once you are retired, many more things come in and go out in monthly units, so it is best to start calculating everything in terms of months. Convert weekly figures to monthly figures by multiplying by 4⅓ (the average number of weeks in a month).

Some things are paid or billed monthly and no further calculations are necessary. However, many are seasonable or erratic. In such cases, find the total for the year and divide by 12. It will be best to have two columns, annual and monthly, for simplicity and as a check. (See Sample #1.)

Now make up the income side of the picture.

b. YOUR INCOME CHECKLIST

Earned income
Employment earnings (gross) before deductions
Part-time earnings
Income from business
Spouse's earnings
Employer's payments on your behalf

Investment income
Bank interest
Bond interest
Stock dividends
Interest on money lent to others
Capital gains

Other sources of income
Rental income
Room rental or boarders
Car-pool income
Hobby items sold
Pension income

Investments or capital items sold and spent
  rather than saved or reinvested
Gambling gains (losses would go under expenses)
Unemployment insurance received
Family contributions
Other

You may not have income under all of these headings, but list every source you have had in the past year. Otherwise it will seem that you received less money than you actually did and so give a false impression of your annual living costs.

When you have completed the income side, compare it to your last income tax return. This will provide a check against any omission. There may be some items you did not include in your tax return, such as your spouse's income — so make adjustments if necessary. Here are some guides for calculating the entries.

The first item is wages. Calculate and use the gross amount for the year before deductions, and divide by 12 for the monthly figures. Net figures after deductions can be confusing. After retirement, most of your income will be gross — that is, you will receive the full amount without deductions being made at the source. You will then pay any taxes due by making quarterly estimated tax payments or, if estimated tax payments are not due, by paying the tax due when you file your income tax return.

Start on this basis now and you can follow it through into your retirement records. The first entry is the gross item from your wage statement, Form W-2 (if employed), divided by 12. If you are self-employed, use your net income from the business, gross receipts minus your expenses related to the business. Exclude any salary or draw you might take.

The next will be income from a second job, if you have one, or from any part-time work you do. Again, take an annual total and calculate the monthly average. As this must be kept on a household basis, record any earnings made by your spouse. This won't be repeated with every item as you go along but, wherever both partners have items of income or expense, list them. It is best to enter them separately and identify each properly so that future checking will be more accurately and easily done.

Now, list investment income: interest on loans due you, savings accounts, bonds, and other investments. Include dividends from stocks and mutual funds. Check if any of your insurance policies or tax shelters pay interest.

If you own rental property, determine your net rental income. This could be income from any property you rent year-round or on a short-term basis. Your net rental income would equal your gross rents minus your rental expenses such as insurance, utilities, pest control, repairs, etc. Do not include depreciation, which is a paper write-off for tax purposes. You want to know how much will actually be left after all rental expenses are paid and, therefore, if you have a mortgage on the property, deduct your mortgage payment which most likely includes principal and interest. This is necessary to arrive at an accurate cash flow amount even though your principal payments are not deducted when computing your net rental income for tax purposes. Keep in mind that you are calculating your income available, which is an exercise slightly different from your tax calculations.

You may have other miscellaneous items. You may have operated a car pool, for example, or sold some craft items at a local show. Everything should be recorded, including gambling winnings or realized capital gains. Losses from gambling or investments (if made up out of current income) are best handled by including them in the expenditures to show where the money went.

The last item catches any remaining income, such as pension income from a trust. If there is any income you have not included under one of the above headings, show it now.

Add it up. Does it look right? If not, first check your addition, then the accuracy of your entries and, finally, if the mistake has not shown up, review each item carefully against your income tax return. When satisfied with the result, you have finished the income side.

To better illustrate the handling of income and expenditures and how they can be manipulated to pay for an enjoyable life in retirement, the incomes, expenditures, and handling of the assets of a hypothetical couple, John and Mary Jones, make up the following sample.

SAMPLE #1
GROSS INCOME WHILE EMPLOYED 199—

ITEM	ANNUAL	MONTHLY
Employment earnings: John	$30,000	$2,500
Employment earnings: Mary	15,000	1,250
Bank interest: John	1,312	109
Bank interest: Mary	875	73
Dividends (joint)	480	40
Earnings from car pool	416	35
TOTAL	$48,083	$4,007

c. HOW DO YOU SPEND YOUR INCOME?

Now you need to list where your income went. Here is a checklist of the main categories to help you get started.

EXPENSES (WHILE EMPLOYED)

Payroll deductions
Income taxes
Pension plan
Union dues
Group insurance
Charity
Life (group) insurance

Housing
Rent
Real estate taxes
Heat
Power, water, telephone
TV rental or cable
Mortgage
Insurance
Repairs and replacements
Maintenance
Furnishings
Appliances

Personal
Food
Laundry and cleaning
Life insurance
Clothing
Vacation
Personal care and spending
Recreation
Reading material
Medical (paid directly, not deducted from payroll earnings)

Dental (paid directly, not deducted
   from payroll earnings)
Public transportation
Gifts and donations

Automobile costs and depreciation

Savings
Seller financed mortgage payments
Investments
Savings
Private pension
Life insurance premiums (if there is an increase
   in cash surrender value)

1. **Payroll deductions**

Start with the payroll deductions. If you are employed, your wage statement will show your gross pay and how much was deducted at the source for insurance, medical plans, company pension plan, income tax, and other items. Your income tax returns will show any additional tax paid or refunds coming to you. If you had a number of employers during the year, or if you were self-employed, your income tax return is the best place to find these figures as they are likely to be accurate. Record them for both you and your spouse as the first group of expenses.

2. **How to calculate the cost of home ownership**

The second, and often the largest single item, is the cost of your dwelling. This may be simple to handle if you rent a house or apartment, but it may be much more complex if you own your home. If you rent, enter the monthly rent, then any other expenses that are not included such as electricity, water, telephone, TV rental, cable, and heat.

If you own your home, rent will not be an entry, but the utilities and the following other expenses will be. The first are the real estate taxes which you can readily ascertain from your tax bill.

The next is the cost of a mortgage. Mortgage payments are generally composed of two or more parts. There are several types of mortgages, but the two most common are the conventional and the amortized. You must first find out what type of mortgage you have and what the payments include. These are probably a combination of principal repayment and interest, perhaps real estate taxes and insurance. You must be able to separate these because the principal repayment is a saving (because you are building equity in your property), but the interest is an expense.

The conventional mortgage often consists of equal monthly payments for the life of the loan: 15, 20, or 30 years. The monthly payments are divided between principal (the loan amount borrowed), and interest. At the end of the loan term, you will have paid the borrowed amount in full assuming that all monthly payments were on time.

Lenders are required to furnish you with an annual statement of mortgage interest paid. However, you need not wait to find out how much principal and interest is paid in a year. If the owner of your mortgage has not already provided you with a table showing you the breakdown of your payments into principal and interest components over the life of the loan, ask for it now.

If you have an adjustable rate mortgage, the payments are inclined to jump up or down depending on how interest rates move. Generally, you start out with an interest rate 3% to 4% below the conventional rate mortgage interest. At a set interval, usually six months to a year, your mortgage payment is adjusted to take into account the current interest rate. An annual cap of usually 2% and a lifetime cap of 6% is common with most adjustable rate mortgages. That means that for any year that you hold your mortgage, the interest rate will not exceed 2% over its current rate, and over the life of the loan, your interest rate will not be more than 6% of the initial rate.

Caps on adjustable rate mortgages are good because they allow you to plan for the maximum jump that your mortgage payment might take when the adjustment period comes around. If you don't plan for this maximum jump, you may be faced with a financial hardship and stand to lose your home if you fail to make your mortgage payments.

If you have a mobile home, you may have the same type of loan used to finance an automobile. However, it doesn't matter what kind it is; the division between interest and principal repayments should be known.

Under mortgage or loan interest, be sure to put the interest payments to be made in the year for which the account is being made up. Farther down, under savings, enter that section of the mortgage or loan payments that is a repayment of the principal.

Next, consider the insurance on your house and perhaps personal property. While this is often referred to as "fire insurance," it frequently protects you against many other risks, such as theft and water damage. Often "personal property" — your clothes, jewelry, furniture, etc. — is included. Read your policy and find out. If you can't understand the wording, ask your agent to explain it. Rather than attempt to separate items into different expenses, record them as one lump sum. If you have a rented home or apartment and do not insure the property but have insurance on your furniture and personal property, include that too.

The expenses for which you are regularly billed are easily ascertained, the estimates are the difficult ones. Soon after a house has been built, repairs are required and these increase over the years. They can range from the simple replacement of washers in leaky faucets to the much more expensive appliance, electrical, or plumbing repairs. Then there is maintenance of the grounds, upkeep, painting, and cleaning. On top of these come the things that may be quite expensive but which will come as surely as the familiar "death and taxes."

Standard roofs have about a 20-year life. Plumbing in older houses, particularly if it is galvanized piping, will have to be replaced. Furnaces and mechanical items will wear out. To estimate these costs, use last year's figures as a guide. If you plan to continue living in your present house, look back over the past few years and see what you have been spending. Then decide if this looks like a reasonable basis on which to project your spending for the next year.

With the estimates and your past experience, you will be able to come up with a reasonably accurate guess. It may be high one year and low the next, but you will be prepared for the expenses as they come for they will average out over the years. If possible, have all major repairs and replacements completed and paid for before retirement.

The next item to consider is heat and air conditioning. If you have an accurate record of past bills, you can use those figures. If you do not, the oil or gas company can tell you your last year's total and whether an increase is forthcoming.

If you are in a condominium or a co-op apartment, rent a mobile home lot, or have some arrangement different from those discussed above, get a figure that covers all the related costs, including such things as membership in the organization.

3. Personal expenses

Start by calculating food costs. If you pay cash for your groceries, you may not have any records, but a little thought can tie it down fairly accurately.

Most families follow a certain shopping routine — perhaps a major trip once a week. Keep all sales slips for each week for one year. Soon you will not only have an accurate figure, but you may also learn some interesting things about controlling your food costs. Remember to add any meals usually purchased away from home to this total.

Estimating clothing expense is more difficult because it doesn't usually follow a regular monthly pattern. If you can, estimate over a period of years the average annual expenditure. Laundry and cleaning bills can be estimated next. Don't forget the seasonal bulges that occur when putting away winter and summer clothes.

4. Automobile costs and depreciation

Automobile costs require thought and accuracy. Perhaps you have a charge account that covers regular running expenses and repairs, tires, batteries, etc. If not, make a very honest estimate here. Adjust for rising prices if necessary.

Now, list installment payments if your car is financed. As with a mortgage, these payments will be a combination of principal repayments and interest. Ask for a breakdown from the finance company. Include the principal repayments as savings; the interest paid goes under expenses.

The annual decrease in your car's value due to aging will be taken care of by depreciation. Depreciation is the estimated decrease in the value of the car during a certain period, say one year, because you have used up some of the car's available mileage and the model is now one year older. It is not a cash cost this year — you paid it out when you bought the car. It simply means that, when sold or traded, the car will bring less than its original price. The difference is the depreciation and, when calculating an annual cost, this figure should be estimated and included.

Accurate records over the years indicate that a car, on average, depreciates at the rate of about 30% per year. That means 30% of its value at the beginning of the year is used up in the year, and this must be subtracted from the value to obtain a figure with which to start the following year. The next depreciation is taken from this reduced figure and, thus, the depreciation declines each year. However, repairs increase often almost as quickly as depreciation declines.

Assume that you are driving a car that cost $12,000. The yearly cost of depreciation is calculated by taking 30% of the value at the beginning of that year. Thus, for the first year it is $3,600. In the second year the calculation is made by deducting the $3,600 from the $12,000, that is, $8,400, and then taking 30% of that, which is $2,520. For the third year and successive years, continue on in the same manner.

Now add in the license, operating, and insurance costs and you have a total for the year.

If you have capital tied up in your car, that money might earn 10% interest or more in investments, so you are foregoing at least 10% income for every $1,000 invested in your car. Keep that in mind for future reference, but do not enter it in this calculation.

Sample #2 shows an example of calculating auto expenses. Replace these figures with your own.

SAMPLE #2
ESTIMATED AUTOMOBILE EXPENSES

Consider a car that cost $8,000 five years ago

Estimated annual driving:
12,000 miles of combined city and country driving

Depreciation	$1,331
License	50
Insurance	750
Gasoline, oil, lubrication, etc.	1,050
Repairs, replacement	275
Total	**$3,456**

Note: If the $8,000 had been invested it might earn $800 per year. If this is considered part of the expense of ownership, it then totals $4,256.

d. THE FINAL LIST

Sample #3 shows how one couple might have used their means; it is not presented as a goal to which you, personally, should strive. The money accumulated during the year would actually be greater than the savings shown in the sample because the automobile expense of $3,456 includes $1,331 for depreciation. This is not money paid out this year but represents the decrease in value of the car during the year. This money should be saved to be available to purchase a new car when the present one is traded in.

SAMPLE #3
HOW THE MONEY WAS SPENT

ITEM	ANNUAL	MONTHLY
Deductions and taxes		
Income tax deducted from pay: John	$4,588	$382
Income tax deducted from pay: Mary	1,509	126
Taxes paid direct	253	21
Other payroll deductions	1,080	90
Utilities		
Power, water, TV rental	650	54
Telephone (home and vacation home)	300	25
Home		
Real estate taxes	1,950	164
Heat	950	79
Repairs and maintenance	775	64
Insurance	525	44
Furnishings	700	58
Appliances	325	27
Vacation home		
Taxes	1,100	93
Insurance	500	542
Power	225	18
Repairs and maintenance	850	71
Personal		
Food and meals	6,125	510
Laundry and cleaning	350	29
Clothing	2,080	173
Vacation	1,100	92
Recreation	1,500	125
Reading	200	17
Personal care	600	500
Medical and dental (not insured)	425	35
Life insurance premium	162	13
Automobile: John	3,456	288
Automobile: Mary	3,456	288
Gifts and donations	400	33
Contributions to 401(K) plan		
John	5,400	450
Mary	2,700	225
Savings	3,849	321
TOTAL	$48,083	$4,957

8
ESTIMATING RETIREMENT INCOME

Now that you have completed a list of last year's earnings and expenditures, you are ready to prepare an estimate of your post-retirement income. You will then have an accurate picture of your financial position and will know what changes, if any, will be necessary.

a. MAINTAINING YOUR STANDARD OF LIVING

Retired people typically need at least 75% of their peak income earnings to maintain their pre-retirement standard of living. Your employer's pension plan probably will not provide that much. And even if social security happens to survive to pay you any retirement benefits, the combination of those benefits and employer-provided pension funds still won't add up to that 75% you need.

Plain and simple, you will need personal savings and wise investments to meet your retirement needs. You need to apply just as much of that current energy that goes into your career, family, and social activities into saving, investing, and planning if you intend to retire well off.

A plan of action that takes into account wealth building, inflation, catastrophic possibilities, and future living expenses has to be devised and implemented. While the process is long and tedious, the rewards are only possible if definite steps are taken systematically and seriously. There are no real short cuts. Forget about the rich uncle, the lottery, or becoming the entrepreneur of the century until such prospects are firmly in hand and no longer just prospects.

Put the entire picture into perspective by asking a few key questions. What will your financial portfolio consist of when you retire? How much in pension money will you receive? What income-producing assets will you need if your pension is not enough?

If you have sources of income from investments that will appreciate, real estate or stocks, pension funds, and earnings from employment, you won't have to commit as much of your current earnings to retirement. You need to determine exactly what you will receive in the way of retirement benefits. You need to find out *today* what you can expect from your company pension plan.

Typically, if you are recently vested (i.e., entitled to receive pension benefits because you have been with the company for a certain number of years) in the company's pension plan, you can expect to receive 10% to 15% of your salary if you retire at age 65. If you work beyond the minimum vesting period, you can expect a larger percentage of your salary. You can figure on 20% to 25% of your salary if you retire after 20 years with your company, and 35% after 30 years. Inflation and salary increases will alter these numbers somewhat, but by using these figures you can, at least, begin assessing your expected company pension.

You should also consider what you will receive from social security even if you are among the growing number of skeptics who doubt its survival as a social program. (See chapter 12 for more on social security.)

b. ASSESSING YOUR NEEDS

To begin, assess your future housing, living, and recreational needs. Try to estimate what you will do during retirement and at what cost. While many of your current expenses will probably be eliminated by the time you retire, or at least shortly after you retire, include every possible expenditure imaginable that you may incur during your retirement.

For example, your mortgage should be paid off or almost paid off by the time you retire. Your children will be educated and out of the house. Most of the luxury items you covet will probably be purchased in the next 10 years, or at least before you retire (assuming you retire around age 60 or so).

You can eliminate commuting and other such job-related expenses if you definitely plan to avoid working after you retire. If you move to a warmer location, your clothing and heating bills will be reduced.

Factor in non-recurring or infrequent purchases such as a new car every five to seven years. The car you own on the day you retire will most likely have to be replaced a few years later. New cars cost more and more every year. What will "your car" cost 10, 20, or 30 years from today?

Another way to arrive at your future money needs is to estimate what your expenses will be in your peak earning years. Use Worksheet #1 to help you arrive at these figures.

You will probably have a bigger house and a slightly more expensive car by then. Your entertainment and clothes expenses may also be slightly higher. Again, don't leave anything out.

WORKSHEET #1
RETIREMENT EXPENDITURES

Name: _____

Years to retirement: _____

Today's date: _____

	Expenditures	
	Now	At retirement
1. Housing*	_____	_____
2. Clothing	_____	_____
3. Food (including tobacco and alcohol)	_____	_____
4. Transportation (including car repair, car payment, gas, etc.)	_____	_____
5. Insurance (life, medical, auto, property, liability, disability)	_____	_____
6. Medical and dental (premiums and expenses)**	_____	_____
7. Taxes (federal, state, local, FICA)	_____	_____
8. Entertainment (dining out, vacations, movies, sports, etc.)	_____	_____
9. Gifts/donations	_____	_____
10. Savings/investments	_____	_____
11. Miscellaneous	_____	_____
TOTAL EXPENDITURES (add lines 1 through 11)	_____	_____

* Probably 25% to 30% less during retirement if mortgage is paid off.
** Plan for a 50% increase due to increased illnesses and insurance costs.

Now, take 75% (60% if you expect to live more modestly when you retire) of each item in your expense list to arrive at what you will probably need upon retirement. Then total those items.

The 75% used here is a reasonable estimate of how much your expenses will be during retirement compared to your standard of living just prior to retirement. If you need to adjust that percentage or certain specific items, by all means do so. Your objective is to come as close as possible to accurately estimating your expenses in retirement.

The next step is to estimate how long you will live during retirement to figure how much in total you will need during those years. To do that, multiply your projected annual budget by how long you can expect to live. (See Table #1.)

TABLE #1
LIFE EXPECTANCY

If your current age is:	Then the average life expectancy for your age group is:	
	Male	Female
60	77.69	82.85
61	78.25	83.03
62	78.56	83.22
63	78.88	83.42
64	79.21	83.63
65	79.57	83.85
66	79.93	84.09
67	80.32	84.33
68	80.72	84.59
69	81.14	84.86
70	81.50	85.14

c. CONSIDER INFLATION

According to the latest U.S. census, life expectancy is increasing. While the average life expectancy is over age 75, more people today are over age 85 than ever before. Thus, we must plan to live a much longer time in retirement than our grandparents did, and, therefore, we must include those additional retirement years in our overall financial plan. Of course, you must adjust your budget to take into account inflation, higher taxes, (income, sales, and property), and at least one major setback, most likely an incapacitating illness.

It is reasonable to expect that inflation will average 5% over the next 25 years. Therefore, your financial needs will need to be adjusted and will look like something shown in Table #2. You can use Worksheet #2 to estimate your annual retirement income taking inflation into account.

TABLE #2
IMPACT OF INFLATION

Spendable income needed during retirement to buy what $10,000 buys at the start of retirement

Number of years after the start of retirement	Inflation rate		
	4%	6%	8%
5	$12,167	$13,382	$14,693
10	14,802	17,908	21,589
15	18,009	23,966	31,722
20	21,911	32,071	46,610
25	26,658	42,919	68,485

d. PLANNING FOR THE UNEXPECTED

You may be surprised by the amount you have estimated that you will need as a minimum to retire well-off. This estimate, however, does not provide for any real upsets in the economy that, if one occurred, would require substantially greater financial resources. You need to ask yourself where that money would come from. If you are just starting on a savings/investment program, you will need to put an added portion away to meet your goal.

e. CONCLUSION

In this chapter we have attempted to estimate what your day-to-day living expenses will be when you retire. You will most likely seek to retain as much as possible of the lifestyle you have come to enjoy even after you retire. You are no longer in the dark about the cost of doing that. What is also abundantly clear is that you must save and invest wisely in order to have the income you will need when you retire. How do you accumulate wealth today when just about everything you currently earn is spent before you earn it? How do you save now when you have yet to increase your standard of living as you would like to? What can you expect from social security? These are the questions addressed in the next few chapters.

WORKSHEET #2
ESTIMATING YOUR ANNUAL
RETIREMENT INCOME

Name: _____

Years to retirement: _____

Today's date: _____

1. Current income from all sources   _____
2. Target retirement income
   (usually 60% to 80% of current
   income)   _____
3. Pension income   _____
4. Social security benefits   _____
5. Amount needed from other sources
   (line 2 minus lines 3 and 4)   _____
6. Annual income from investments   _____
7. Employment income (part-time
   or self-employment)   _____

8. Total expected retirement income
   (Add lines 3, 4, 6, and 7.
   This amount should equal line 2.)   _____

   Adjustment for inflation after retirement:
   2% real rate of return — earnings above inflation

9. 5 years: multiply line 8 by 1.403   _____
10. 10 years: multiply line 8 by 1.967   _____
11. 15 years: multiply line 8 by 2.759   _____

9
YOUR COST OF LIVING IN RETIREMENT

With your estimate of retirement income in hand, you can now decide what you can afford. You need to know how you are going to live and the cost of your choices. The changes made in your way of living may make a significant difference in your expenses. For example, some employment related costs will be eliminated (e.g., the cost of transportation to and from work, union dues, pension payments, etc.), and you will benefit from discounts offered to seniors.

The list of expenditures you made while working is out of date because of these changes, but it will provide basic, valuable information for making decisions now. The first step is to list your expected expenses in retirement, using the figures of your present costs as a guide, but adjusting each for changes that can be predicted. We will examine these to see what to expect.

a. INCOME TAX RESPONSIBILITIES

If 75% or more of your income has been from employment, income tax has probably been deducted at the source and any balance due must be paid when your annual return is due without regard to any extensions of time to file. However, now, if your income comes from sources from which withholding has not been made, and it probably will after retirement, you are required to make quarterly estmated tax payments if you are liable for over $499 in taxes after subtracting tax payments and credits from your total tax liability.

An exception to making estimated tax payments will apply if either your other tax payments plus credits are *at least* 90% of your actual liability *or* you made withholding payments of at least 100% of the tax on your return filed for the previous tax year. For example, if in 1990 your withholding is $10,000, which is at least equal to your 1989 tax liability, no estimated tax payments are due even though your 1990 tax liability may exceed $10,000.

You would be wise to discuss these possible liabilities with a tax advisor to avoid underpayment penalties. If you do not have such a connection, do not hesitate to contact your local tax office. They are most helpful and you have nothing to fear as they will give all information freely without asking your name. They are courteous and try to assist as much as possible.

Warning: Approaching the tax office on simple matters is all right but be wary of seeking advice on more complex matters. Because of the complexities of the income tax laws, it is best to seek expert advice.

b. DO NOT LET THEM LAPSE!

Once you are retired, the benefits your employer deducted from your paycheck cease and you must reinstate them directly if you wish them to continue. You may have been receiving extra coverage through extended hospital, dental, or drug plans, which, again, will lapse if you do not pay the premiums. You also may have had optional life insurance coverage that you will want to continue after you retire. You should be sure to ask your employer for all the pertinent information about these matters before you leave work to ensure that your post-retirement benefits continue uninterrupted.

c. YOUR HOME

The next cost to consider is your dwelling. If you continue to live in the same home, you can simply use the expense calculations made in your first schedule with any estimate for expected changes. If you move later, you can make the change in a final calculation.

Some municipalities have special property tax abatements for owners above a certain age. Check to see if yours has this provision.

In making your forecast of retirement plans, you should realize that advancing years may require some difference in your estimate. Will you be able to continue to do some of the heavier chores (e.g., snow removal and lawn care)? If not, include the cost of having someone do them for you.

d. EATING FOR HEALTH AND PLEASURE

Eating can be a most enjoyable experience, yet retired people who are not usually cooking to please a hungry family often lose interest in food. As a result, they may rely on tea and toast or similar easily prepared things. By doing so, they lose the opportunity of having an enjoyable experience, and they may not get the necessary nourishment required to maintain health.

Younger people eat more and, therefore, are more likely to get all the protein, minerals, and vitamins required along with the calories to provide the energy needed. The older person requires fewer calories for energy, but still needs at least as much of the other nutrients as before. As you reduce the quantity of food eaten, you may need a better selection; this is still possible with simple, easily prepared meals.

The starting point is finding out whether your current diet is adequate. There are several ways of doing this: ask your doctor for suggestions and advice, call your local health office and ask if there is a qualified nutritionist or nurse available who can provide the information, or read some of the excellent material available either from the health office or the library. You may find that by reading you can make up new, interesting, enjoyable meals, keep control of costs, and add a new zest to eating.

Now that you have the time, why not make this a project and see how much pleasure it can provide? Try new things and look at cooking as a source of pleasure rather than a chore. Rapidly increasing food costs may be a problem, and using replacements for the very high-cost items may be a good way to control them; shop to take advantage of specials or items in season when they cost less. Remember, the aim is not just to cut cost, but to eat well and enjoyably at the same time. By planning and buying carefully, you may be able to have some of those things that you really enjoy, even if they are high priced.

Dining out is less expensive at lunch, and often the menu is lighter and more suitable for seniors. Why not invite a friend and make it a social outing too? Some retired people find pleasure in forming a small dinner club that meets regularly. It is an event to look forward to and a chance to eat someone else's cooking. Retired men often take a new interest in cooking; they may become experts and take great pleasure in preparing dishes that appeal to them.

The opportunities are there: make eating a pleasure, and at the same time provide the nourishment you need for your health and happiness.

e. CLOTHING

Clothing costs also may be reduced, for work often requires a standard of dress you need not maintain during retirement. You may have the time to make some of your clothes now, which will save you substantial funds and provide you with an interesting hobby at the same time. Once again, the changes made depend on your personal circumstances, so make the best estimate you can. Laundry and cleaning costs may also be reduced.

f. ENTERTAINMENT

You may wish to spend more time with hobbies and enjoy additional entertainment because you have more time available, but this doesn't mean you need to spend more money. First, you no longer need to go to shows at the expensive times, like Friday and Saturday nights. You can go on "off" nights and to matinees. Rather than going out for dinner, you and your friends might enjoy a leisurely lunch. Now that you have more time, you may do more entertaining at home as well. Further, you will save by taking advantage of the lower prices so often given to seniors. Also look into special group rates.

g. VACATIONS AND TRAVEL

There are many basic savings now available to you in the travel area.

(a) Select off-peak season dates which are usually substantially cheaper.

(b) Notice that certain days of departure and return are often much less expensive on airlines and other carriers.

(c) Consider vacation periods that are often not possible for the working person and may be more reasonably priced.

(d) Resorts may give a discount if it is requested. Inquire; you shouldn't pay full price when it is not necessary.

(e) Public carriers often give reduced rates to seniors.

(f) Look for less expensive rather than the glamour spots. For example, in winter, accommodation on the northern gulf coast of Florida often costs as little as one-quarter of a similar place farther south.

(g) Look for less expensive group plans.

h. ELIMINATE INSTALLMENT PAYMENTS

Installment payments are generally used to purchase larger, more expensive items of furniture, clothing, or, perhaps, an automobile. At this stage in your life, it may be that you will have the option of delaying such purchases. While installment purchases may be desirable, or necessary, they often include an interest charge at a very high rate.

Now the desire to eliminate unnecessary costs and obtain the most for every dollar calls for the end of expensive borrowing. Save for major purchases, but if you do borrow, do so on the best security you have to obtain the lowest rate.

i. MEDICAL COVERAGE

Generally, if you are eligible for social security, retirement, or disability benefits, you are eligible for

Medicare, a federal health insurance program administered by your local Social Security Administration office. There are limits, however, on the hospital and medical coverage provided by Medicare. For example, Medicare does not cover eyeglasses, routine dental care, nursing home care, and prescription drugs. Therefore, you might want to buy supplemental health insurance that will pick up health care coverage where Medicare stops. Some employer health plans allow you to continue coverage at your cost under their plans when you retire. Check with your employer and/or appropriate health insurance carrier about full medical protection and the cost to you after you retire.

j. TRANSPORTATION

Now that travel requirements such as going to work and driving children about are past, many of you can take a new look at transportation requirements. The operating cost of an automobile is very high, and many "two-car" couples find they are able to manage with one car during retirement. Others dispose of cars completely; public transportation is often less expensive and almost all public carriers give discounts to pensioners. Airlines and railways have discounts at certain times. The combined use of public transportation and rental cars for special occasions may be satisfactory. Consider these factors again if you decide to relocate your home.

If you do decide to keep your automobile, costs will follow the same basic calculations made previously but, if you have driven to work, you will now automatically eliminate this driving. However, do not underestimate the rapidly escalating costs of running an automobile. Retired people often make a basic change in automobile usage and, therefore, in the annual cost. This may be possible if you foresee a substantial reduction in mileage. In addition to gasoline and oil, repairs and replacements are closely related to mileage. Depreciation is quite high in the early years but it decreases rapidly over time. Insurance, license, garage, and other similar expenses, however, will remain constant.

The simple reduction of your mileage may substantially reduce the annual running costs. If, for example, you now expect to cut your mileage in half, you could keep the car twice as long, and your average annual depreciation would be much lower.

If you reduce your mileage to 5,000 miles per year by eliminating that drive to work, and you are able to keep your car twice as long or until it has gone 50,000 miles (a 10-year period), your average depreciation would be reduced by half each year.

With just you and your spouse using the car and the need to cut costs, it might be best for you to purchase a smaller car that requires less gasoline. As well, a less expensive car will have a lower depreciation rate and lower operating costs.

k. BANK CHARGES

Most banks will grant discounts for some services to people over 60. These often include a discount for depositors renting safety deposit boxes, free checking privileges, a bonus on interest earned to help keep up with inflation, and no service charge for some utility bill payments. Ask your manager what discounts or free services are available to you.

l. EVALUATE EACH EXPENDITURE AGAIN

Now total your expected expenses and compare them with the anticipated income. How does it look? Is your income adequate? If it is and you have listed all the things you wish to do, there is no problem. However, if there is not enough income to cover the expenses or there are still things that you had hoped to be able to afford but you did not include, you should now investigate the possible ways of increasing income and reducing expenditures, eliminating those items that provide little satisfaction. There are plenty of opportunities to make painless adjustments.

It is time you reviewed each expenditure seriously and judged it by your new lifestyle. Does it make a worthwhile contribution to the welfare and happiness of you and your spouse now that you are retired?

When you review your list again, challenge every item and justify each carefully. If you cannot, eliminate it.

10
HOW TO INCREASE YOUR RETIREMENT INCOME

Today, the choices are vast when it comes to selecting what you should do with your money and how to protect it. There are thousands of products and investment opportunities. Some of them are safe; others are very risky. As a retired person, your best choices will most likely be the safe, conservative ones. In all cases, any investment that you participate in should answer three basic questions:

(a) How much risk is involved?

(b) How liquid is the investment?

(c) Does it meet your financial goals?

Risk means the likelihood of your getting your money back. The higher the risk, the greater the chance of your losing your money. Conversely, low risk means that your principal will most likely be returned to you under the terms of the investment agreement. Generally, if you are going to put your money at great risk, the potential reward should be great. Don't go into high-risk investments for a return that can be achieved with less risk.

The best investment strategy is to diversify. By spreading your money among several investments (e.g., money market accounts, real estate, stocks, and bonds), you reduce the risk of your investment program. But no matter what, as a retired individual, your level of risk should be in the low or medium categories. Holding high-risk investments during retirement is unwise because you can't afford to jeopardize a financially safe retirement at this late date.

a. SAFE INVESTMENTS

Your primary goal as a retired person should be the conservation of income and principal. There are numerous investments that will help you achieve this goal. The yields, return on investment, may not be as great as other higher-risk investments, but your money will be fairly safe.

A balanced, capital preservation program for your retirement funds could be as follows:

(a) Money market account: 30%

(b) Bonds (high quality): 40%

(c) Growth stocks (high quality): 20%

(d) Real estate: 10%

Savings deposits, money market accounts, and certificates of deposit (CDs) placed with a federally insured bank, savings and loan, or credit union are low-risk investments. Also low-risk are government securities such as treasury bills, notes, or bonds.

Money placed in banks and savings and loan institutions that are insured by the Federal Deposit Insurance Corporation (FDIC) and the Federal Savings and Loan Insurance Corporation (FSLIC) provide a guarantee by the government that up to $100,000 per bank, per person (not account) is protected. The National Credit Union Administration (NCUA) guarantees credit union funds of up to $100,000 per account.

Because your money in these federally insured accounts is safe up to a fixed amount, you should limit your funds per bank or credit union so you don't exceed that limit. Should your account exceed the maximum amount insured, it would be wise to move some of your money to another federally insured financial institution.

Warning: Never assume your financial institution is insured because not all of them are. Ask before you invest.

1. Savings accounts

Currently, a typical bank savings account pays 5¼% interest per year. What you need to pay particular attention to is not only the rate of interest, but how that interest is being calculated (i.e., simple or compound).

Simple interest provides a lower yield than compound interest. For example, $10,000 at 10% simple interest yields only $1,000 after one year. If your account compounded the interest, you will earn in a year $1,051.56 on a daily compound, $1,050.65 on a weekly compound, or $1,047.13 on a monthly compound.

Passbook savings accounts have been the preferred choice for many investors. You can walk into any neighborhood bank and open an account. With few or no restrictions, you can withdraw funds at your convenience.

2. Money market accounts and
   money market funds

Money market accounts are deemed a step above passbook savings accounts. They are just as safe as other accounts placed in federally insured financial institution, and they pay a higher yield than savings accounts.

With the money invested, the bank lends those funds on a short-term basis (usually 60 to 100 days) to the federal, state, and local government. Some money market funds are also loaned to corporations, banks, and foreign entities. The safest money market accounts tend to be those that limit their lending to the U.S. government because the government guarantees to pay its debt.

Money market accounts are extremely convenient. While they tend to be savings vehicles, most come with check writing privileges and funds can be withdrawn at any time.

Some money market accounts charge monthly maintenance fees. An additional charge may also be imposed if your account falls below a certain minimum balance. To get the most out of your money market account, sign up for one that does not impose these hidden charges. Otherwise, the earnings advantage that you thought you were getting may be lost.

Money market funds work in much the same way as bank money market accounts. Your money market fund may or may not be insured depending on the company with which you invest. If you seek an insured fund, expect the yield to be less than an uninsured one.

Some mutual fund companies impose a sales charge when you invest in one of their funds. Investigate any and all fees that you may be subject to before opening a money market mutual fund.

3. **Certificates of deposit**

If you are willing to lock up your money for a specified period (e.g., six months or a year), you can often get an even higher yield with a certificate of deposit (CD) account. As with savings accounts and money market accounts, CDs purchased at a federally insured institution are a safe investment.

Generally, the earnings rate of a CD is tied to the current interest rate at the time you purchase it. That rate generally will apply over the life of the CD. Consequently, you do lose the flexibility of moving your money should interest rates increase or a greater investment opportunity come along. If you withdraw your funds prior to the end of the CD term, an early withdrawal penalty is usually imposed. This penalty could cancel the earnings you expected.

For greater flexibility, some banks offer CDs with a "teaser" rate, which is tied to the stock market, gold index, or some other measure. Since your primary objective is safety, stay away from the hype. For example, a teaser rate CD may offer a higher rate for the first month to get you to sign up. The rate for the remainder of the term may not be comparable to a rate at another bank. Go for safety and the best overall return.

Many banks will automatically roll over your CD when it matures into another CD for the same period as the original one. This procedure may not work to your advantage. The rate for the new CD may be lower than what you'd like, or you may have other plans for those funds. To avoid tying your money up under a bank rollover procedure, notify your bank in writing before your CD matures that you do not intend to invest the funds in another CD.

4. Federal Treasury investments

The safest investment, by far, is a federal obligation: Treasury bond, bill, or note. Both the payment of the principal and the interest is guaranteed by the federal government plus the interest is exempt from state and local taxes. They can be purchased, without a fee, directly from one of the 12 Federal Reserve banks or from one of their branches in two dozen cities.

The biggest considerations when purchasing a government security after the yield are the period to maturity and the purchase price. U.S. savings bonds can be purchased for as little as $25. Treasury bills, in contrast, require a minimum investment of $10,000. Treasury bonds and notes maturing in over four years can be purchased for a minimum of $1,000.

Treasury bills, commonly referred to as T-bills, mature in three, six, or twelve months. Notes mature from one to ten years depending on the denomination. Bonds, not to be confused with U.S. savings bonds, mature in greater than ten years. Savings bonds mature in ten to twelve years depending on the series.

Because of the different maturity dates of government instruments, it is best to stagger their maturity period so that you do not end up with a huge pile of money at one time. But, be aware that if you need to redeem your government investment before the maturity period, a penalty in the form of a discounted price will probably apply.

Quasi-federal organizations also offer safe investments. The Government National Mortgage Association (Ginnie Mae), the Federal National Mortgage Association (Fannie Mae), and the Federal Home Loan Mortgage Corporation (Freddie Mac) offer securities that are backed by the U.S. government. These investments allow you to invest in a pool of mortgages. As an investor, you receive a portion of the mortgage payment made by hundreds of homeowners on a monthly basis.

Unlike other government securities, the amount of your payment may vary from month to month depending on the number of outstanding mortgages with an agency at any point and time. To compensate for such investment payout uncertainty, these securities are often sold with higher interest rates than treasury securities with the same maturity.

The minimum investment for a Ginnie Mae, Fannie Mae, or Freddie Mac is $25,000. If that amount is too steep, try a mutual fund that invests in these securities. A much lower minimum will be required: $100 to $1,000.

b. MUTUAL FUNDS

Mutual funds can be an excellent alternative to owning stocks, bonds, and money accounts outright. As an investor in a mutual fund, you participate in a variety of investments, not just one, thereby providing diversity under one umbrella. The professional management team that guides your money through the ups and downs of the financial arena watches your investment daily, which is something that investors are not prepared to do.

Mutual funds provide numerous investment options. There are growth funds, income funds, special industry funds, international funds, etc. What fund you choose is completely up to you. What you should strive for is a fund or several funds that have performed relatively well in good times as well as bad times. Choosing a fund of this type will provide some assurance that the fund managers are skilled at providing a good return when the financial market experiences a downturn.

Some funds charge a fee, commonly known as a load, for putting your money in the fund. The fees run from nothing to 8.5%. There are usually annual management fees as well, between 1% and 1.5%. Or you may see a back-end fee, which is imposed when you withdraw any of your investment.

A no-load fund where a sales charge is not imposed is not always the best investment. You need to concentrate on the fund's total return after all fees have been considered. Many load funds provide a far greater total return for the same dollars than some no-load funds. Thus, the bottom line may be more attractive with a loaded fund even after considering the fees than a lower-yielding no-load fund.

Risk is just as important a consideration in a mutual fund as it is with any investment. Do not be lulled into believing that because your money is in a mutual fund your investment is shielded from market risk. Not so! Stick to those investments that provide income and moderate growth with the least amount of risk.

The less risky funds for retirees tend to be growth and income funds, commonly known as balanced funds. These funds invest in companies with great growth potential and add bonds and other income investments to provide a steady stream of income.

Most of the information about a fund can be found in its prospectus, which you should obtain and read. However, consult other outside sources that rate funds and tell you how well your choice has done over several years.

You may want to choose a fund company that offers a family of funds. You can often move your money around within this family of funds by just placing a telephone call. This service is greatly appreciated by many investors who like to take advantage of the changing financial markets.

After selecting your mutual funds, next decide if you want the earning reinvested in additional shares in the fund. As long as you are satisfied with the fund's performance, it may be better to let your money simply ride in that fund. You eliminate having to decide where to put those earnings.

Another benefit of reinvesting the earnings is dollar cost averaging. You purchase shares at different times, and, therefore, at different prices. When the fund dips in value, as it will do at some point, you will pick up more shares. On the other hand, when the value of the fund rises, your earnings purchase fewer shares. Overall, your total cost per share is averaged.

c. STOCKS AND BONDS

If you choose to bypass mutual funds and buy stocks and bonds individually, you should still shoot for diversification among conservative, blue chip companies. Purchase an assortment of companies to minimize your risk. Choose companies that you feel good about, but select them among several industries. Avoid highly volatile stocks where you could lose a large portion of your investment in as little as an hour should the value of the stock plummet.

The same holds true for bonds. Select a good mix whether you are buying corporate or municipal bonds. Know what the bond's rating is as provided by either Moody's or Standard and Poor's, both of which are reporting companies that analyze data about the financial strength of companies and government entities that issue bonds. The safest bonds are those with an A or better rating. Those bonds with less than an A rating may provide a higher yield, but they also provide greater risk. Your local library should have bond rating information available.

You should understand that as interest rates rise, no matter how sound your bond is, the value of your bond goes down. Why? If rates rise, you are holding a bond that is yielding less than what can be purchased in the current bond market. Who will buy your bond if they can buy one with a better yield? Conversely, your bond becomes more valuable when interest rates decrease because now you are holding a product that has a higher yield than those currently being sold.

To reduce the risk associated with bonds, stagger the maturity dates of your investment. Have one come due every year or every other year.

d. OTHER INVESTMENTS

Insurance products such as single premium deferred annuities (SPDA) or immediate annuities offer retirees steady income at low risk for a set amount. An SPDA can be purchased for $5,000 for a payout some time in the future. The earnings, which may be fixed or variable, are accumulated in an SPDA on a tax-deferred basis. The fixed annuity provides less risk with many insurers offering a guaranteed minimum rate.

If you need an immediate income stream, an immediate annuity may be your answer. Your monthly income begins right away, but the amount depends on your age, sex, amount invested, and how long you elect to receive income.

A straight life annuity pays you a monthly check until you die. An installment-refund annuity guarantees that you or your beneficiary will receive at least what your investment equalled. An annuity known as life and period-certainty pays you or your beneficiary for a guaranteed period of time. A joint and survivor payout choice pays you and your beneficiary until both are dead.

Regardless of the annuity or stream of income you want, it is imperative that you shop around before making your investment. Buy an annuity from a financially sound company, one that is A rated by those in the insurance industry. A.M. Best is one example of a rating agency for insurance companies.

11
COPING WITH INFLATION

a. THE SQUEEZE — RISING LIVING COSTS, LOWER INCOME

The problems caused by inflation are well known; living costs rise and those on fixed incomes cannot buy as much. However, during the period of sharply rising prices in the seventies and early eighties, interest rates also rose rapidly, easing the situation for those with money to invest. Today, the buzz words are recession and stagnation with some economists pointing to a full-fledged recession in the early nineties. Increases in the consumer price index (CPI), the retail price measuring rod, and the producer price index (PPI), which measures wholesales prices, point to the continuation of increased costs to the end user, the consumer. The net result is that retired people are being financially squeezed.

Inflation simply reduces what you are able to buy tomorrow with today's dollars. To understand the problem and its effect, divide 72 by the rate of inflation; the result indicates the number of years it will take to cut the purchasing power of a dollar in half.

For example, the CPI in 1982 was as high as 12.8%. But if this rate had continued, the cost of living would have doubled in five and a half years. Fortunately the inflation rate turned down to 4% and now is running at about 5%. But even at that rate, the cost of living will double in approximately 16 years. If that occurs, most of the people retiring today will see the cost of living double in their lifetimes.

What will the future bring? Economists disagree, although most expect inflation to continue. If the cost of living increases, will your income, most of it fixed when you retire, increase at the same rate? For some people it will; for most it will not. Therefore, it is important that you form a plan to enable you to maintain a satisfactory standard of living under inflationary conditions.

b. INTEREST RATES

Both as an investor and a consumer, you must be prepared to cope with rising interest rates. That can best be achieved by managing your debt — adjustable rate mortgages and credit cards. The Federal Reserve Board often responds to rising inflation by increasing interest rates. The theory is that if money is tightened and fewer dollars are chasing goods, prices will not rise as fast.

It's good to control inflation, but what happens to your debt that is tied to the interest rate? If it goes up, so does your debt payment. Those with fixed mortgages or debt are not subject to this unpredictable interest roller coaster.

If you do not have low, unalterable debt rates, you should pay off that adjustable debt as soon as possible. Credit cards with usually the highest debt rate up to 22% should be your first debt-cutting priority. If you have a home equity loan with an adjustable rate, you should pay it back as soon as possible. As rates come down at least 2% lower than your current interest rate, consider refinancing a debt and switching to a fixed rate. Retirees often cannot afford to take on increased debt payments.

The best investments often depend on which way interest rates are expected to go in the future, a difficult thing to guess. No doubt they will fluctuate as they have always done. Consequently, the best thing to do is to make an investment that you will be satisfied with regardless of the direction of interest rates.

Consider the following before putting your money in interest rate sensitive investments such as CDs, bonds, or money market accounts:

(a) Rates paid on money market accounts or treasury securities may change quickly, moving up or down with basic interest rates.

(b) The day after you tie up your money in a CD, the interest rate could go up, causing you to wish you had waited for that higher rate. Or the interest rate could drop, causing you to rejoice that you got a better deal.

(c) Certain contractual obligations, such as bonds, have a stipulated interest rate that will be paid as specified until the maturity date. What is not certain is what that bond will be worth if you sell it before its maturity date. The value of the bond will increase or decrease as interest rates move regardless of the certainty of the interest payment due you.

(d) Other investments, such as common stocks, pay a dividend that the directors set periodically, which may remain the same as last time, be omitted, or increased. There are also "floating rate" securities that pay a rate related to the bank rate and rise and fall with it. Most of these can be sold and the money spent or reinvested.

(e) Pensions and annuities usually pay at a set rate, but interest rates certainly do have an impact on some.

With this information, you should separate into categories that income that is beyond your control, such as social security benefits, and what you can manipulate for the best return on your investment. Keep in mind that you want to take advantage of rising interest rates.

c. INVESTMENTS WITH INFLATION HEDGE

At this stage of your life, safety of your investment must be the most important consideration, and you should only risk funds that could be lost without serious consequences. A younger person has time to make up losses; you do not.

Prior to the October, 1987 stock market crash, it seemed as if every stock or bond was a sure winner certain to produce a profit. As that bleak period in investment history showed, a slowing economy is a time for caution. Even yet, there are some safe, inflation-beating investments for your portfolio (see chapter 10).

1. Real estate

While property values in many parts of the country have out-paced inflation, there are those who predict it will not beat inflation in the 1990s. And, in fact, housing prices have flattened and even declined in some areas. However, according to the National Association of Realtors, there will be some local real estate opportunities.

If you own a home, consider it a good source of income. For example, you are entitled to a special tax-free benefit if you sell your home after you reach age 55. If you decide to sell, you can use those tax-free proceeds to buy a smaller convenient home and invest the unused portion of the sales proceeds. The amount not put into another home will provide additional income. This is discussed further in chapter 14.

2. Art, jewels, antiques, coins, and stamps

Many knowledgeable people and corporations consider items in this category as one of the finest hedges against inflation. They do not produce an income and gain would only be realized through their eventual sale at a profit. You may have some such items that have become much more valuable than you realize, so do not dispose of anything that might fall into this classification without having it valued.

If you do find you have valuable personal property, you should balance the need for current cash against the possibility of getting a higher price later on when you might need it more. Perhaps you have collected these things as a hobby and would prefer to enjoy them as long as possible. At a later date a specific need, a desire for a trip, or some other expenditure might become the deciding factor in selling.

A good example of this is the husband and wife who had both been interested in antiques for years and had built up a fine collection. It was largely in the form of furniture and ornaments they furnished the home with. When the husband retired, an antique dealer visited and offered to buy the house and contents, thus providing a substantial cash sum to augment the owners' pensions. The couple's answer was no. They had an adequate income and, if inflation continued, these things would probably increase in value too. If more cash was needed at any time, they could obtain it by selling the antiques piece by piece. Now the couple are enjoying living with their treasures and remembering with satisfaction their pleasure in finding, purchasing, and often refinishing the pieces.

d. REVERSE MORTGAGES

Some banks offer older persons the opportunity to borrow from the equity in their homes without making any current mortgage payments. With a reverse mortgage, a bank or lending institution pays the borrower a certain amount each month tied to the appreciation in the property. The loan is repaid when the borrower sells the property or dies (your estate pays off the loan).

Before entering into a reverse mortgage, consider these factors:

(a) How much additional income will you receive?

(b) What are the costs associated with such a mortgage?

(c) How long do you plan to live in your home?

(d) What impact will a reverse mortgage have on what you intend to leave to your children or heirs?

(e) How much appreciation will you have to surrender?

Whatever you do with your home, have a trusted advisor, probably an attorney who specializes in real estate matters, review any and all documents of sale or finance before you sign on the dotted line.

e. "THE HEDGE"

Inflation has been prevalent in Europe and South America for so long that people there have learned to mistrust paper money or fixed-value securities and favor the ownership of tangible things like land, buildings, precious metals, gems, and art objects, which are considered a hedge. Such a hedge can be anything that is in limited supply, has a production and distribution cost, is in demand, and for which the value will, hopefully, increase along with a scarcity value or the general price level. If the value does increase, the item can be sold for cash and its increase in value will provide the extra money to purchase as much of other commodities at the higher price as could have been bought with the cash at the time when the hedge was purchased.

If you simply held cash during the period of price rise, that cash would purchase less at the end than at the beginning. The hedge, by increasing in value as inflation progresses, is designed to prevent this.

12
SOCIAL SECURITY

The major source of income for most older Americans is the social security program. Social security was established by Congress in 1935 to provide retirement income and disability benefits for millions of Americans. Today, retirees receive not only retirement benefits but also medical coverage.

You should apply for your benefits a few months before you actually retire. Be prepared to provide your social security card, birth certificates for you and your children, and last earnings record (either form W-2, wage statement, or your self-employment income on your last year's tax return).

The key to social security is protecting and receiving your entitlement to the maximum benefit allowable, which requires planning and monitoring your social security account.

a. ELIGIBILITY

Under the social security system, you must have worked a set number of credits to qualify for benefits. A maximum of four credits per year can be earned. If you were born after 1928, you need at least 40 credits to be fully insured for social security benefits. The number of credits needed to qualify for social security benefits varies for those born between 1914 and 1928. No benefits can be paid to you or your family until the minimum credit requirements are met.

Your monthly benefit is determined by the Primary Insurance Amount (PIA). The benefit is based on your earnings throughout your participation in the social security system. Earnings means gross wages and not just net take-home pay. It includes wages, bonuses, commissions, vacation pay, severance pay, and cash tips of $20 or more. Certain non-cash payments such as the provision of meals or living quarters are also included. The more wages you earn, the greater your PIA. At age 65, you receive 100% of your PIA each month.

If you have made the maximum social security base salary over the past 29 years — currently $45,000 — you are entitled to the maximum benefit of $10,296 in 1990.

Low wage earners get a break when it comes to figuring their PIA. If you earned between $10,000 and $12,000 a year for the maximum number of quarters, you will receive at age 65 about half of your take-home pay at the time of your retirement.

If you postpone receiving social security benefits after age 65, you will receive an extra benefit amount when you do retire — as much as 8% over what you would have received.

b. FAMILY ENTITLEMENT

The social security system allows the following entitlements to family members:

(a) A non-working spouse will receive about 50% of your benefits at age 65 if he or she does not collect his or her own social security benefits.

(b) Your children may also receive social security benefits if you are retired and receiving benefits. Your unmarried child under age 18 (age 19 if a full-time student) and your unmarried child age 18 and over who is disabled and was disabled before age 22, will receive benefits through your entitlement.

(c) Divorced spouses may also receive social security benefits if your marriage lasted at least 10 years.

(d) In some instances, your grandchildren may receive social security benefits based on your participation in the social security system.

c. WORKING AFTER RETIREMENT

If you continue to work after you begin receiving social security benefits, you may lose some of your benefits. If you earn over $8,880 and you are over 65, you lose $1 for every $3 earned. The earnings limit if you are under age 65 is $6,480. There is no earnings limit for retirees over age 70. Also, earnings do not include interest, dividends, pension income, insurance, or rental income.

A special rule provides for unlimited earnings in the year you retire. As an employee, the controlling factor is when you earned the money, not when the wages were paid. If you are self-employed, the primary consideration is whether you are actively involved in your business. Less than 15 hours a month is not considered substantial.

d. EARLY RETIREMENT

Those retiring before age 65 will receive less than 100% of their PIA. Between now and the year 2000, expect to receive only 80% of your PIA. Should you retire after

2000 but before you are 65, expect to receive only 70% of your PIA. This reduced benefit is permanent, taking into account the longer number of years that you are expected to receive benefits.

Beginning in 2009, full benefits are available at age 66 and at 67 in 2027. Age 70 will most likely be the normal retirement age in the future. Thus, if you retire at age 65 in the future you will receive less than full benefits under the early retirement payout.

e. ACCURATE ACCOUNT

According to the General Accounting Office (GAO), the social security files are a mess. It has found discrepancies in 3.5 million records. As many as 9.7 million workers are missing contributions made on their behalf from their accounts. That adds up to $90 billion of unclaimed and misdirected social security funds. As a retiree entitled to social security benefits, with such chaos in the system, you may not be receiving all that you are due.

One way to avoid a possible mix-up is to do a "social security check-up." You should ascertain exactly what is in your social security account now and begin correcting any discrepancies you discover. Contact your local social security office and request Form 7004PC "Request for Statement of Earnings." Upon submitting this completed form, the social security administration will provide you with a detailed account of how much has been credited to your account. Don't be surprised if you happen to disagree with their report. More important, take immediate action to get your account corrected. And, after you have done that, make sure that your retirement benefits that you are entitled to as a result of pointing out an error are adjusted accordingly.

f. TAXES

Social security earnings became subject to taxation in 1984 for high-income taxpayers. Now, up to one-half of your benefits may be subject to federal and state taxes. Your benefits are taxable up to the lesser of either one-half of your annual social security payments or one-half of your income over $32,000 for married couples ($25,000 for single taxpayers).

g. MEDICARE

Generally, if you are eligible for social security benefits and are over age 65, you are eligible for medicare benefits. Part A, hospital coverage, is automatic. Part B, medical and doctor's coverage, is optional.

If you are not eligible for social security, you can still receive coverage under the medicare system. Under Part A, for $156 a month you can receive hospital coverage with a $560 annual deductible. You must be a U.S. citizen or have lived in the U.S. for at least five years to qualify for medicare without the social security benefits. Part B, medical and doctor's coverage, costs $31.90 a month.

Medicare does not cover all nursing home costs, which can be as high as $25,000 a year or more. Medicare pays for nursing home stays that are staffed by doctors and nurses. The nursing home admission must follow a hospital stay. Coverage is limited to 100 days per admission. Retirees should not count on medicare entirely for their medical costs needs and should investigate long-term care insurance that will pick up where medicare leaves off.

13
PUT YOUR AFFAIRS IN ORDER

a. LEGAL MATTERS

Everyone has had the experience of looking for something that he or she is certain is around somewhere but can't find. Years later, it turns up in some unexpected place. This may have caused expense, an opportunity lost, or other problems. Should anything happen to you, how will others find your necessary and valuable papers? There is a simple answer: keep them all together in a secure yet easily found place, make a record of them all, and tell several people where they are kept.

Which documents are important?

(a) Your birth certificate (required for insurance and other purposes)

(b) Your social security number (for pensions and many financial matters)

(c) Your marriage certificate (to certify the legal position of your spouse or children)

(d) A list of any safety deposit boxes and their location, box and key numbers (they are not the same), and the location of the keys

(e) All securities you own and their location (It is generally advisable to have them registered.) Keep the purchase invoices, if they are available, and attach to the certificate to establish cost for capital gains or losses. If you do not have them, list cost prices and attach any supporting evidence such as canceled checks, records, and correspondence.

(f) The location and date of your current will so that no one will act on an earlier, outdated one

(g) All your insurance policies and their location (fire, life, etc.)

(h) Details of property ownership, cost, mortgages, location of deed, tax bills, etc.

(i) Leases, if any

(j) Debts

(k) Any other legal papers of significance

(l) A statement of any powers of attorney you have granted and your living will if you have one

(m) Burial plans, if you have made them

1. Power of attorney

A power of attorney is valuable should you become seriously ill or incapacitated and unable to act on your own behalf. If this occurs, those caring for you either will not be able to do anything with respect to transactions, such as the sale of securities, which officially require your sanction, or will have to go through the cumbersome and expensive process of obtaining a court order to act for you. Both spouses should have one, as both signatures are required on some legal documents.

A properly executed power of attorney gives someone the power to act on your behalf in such cases. Obviously, this authority should be granted only after very careful consideration and to a person or people whom you can trust completely. Each state has its own laws regarding powers of attorney.

Even if you are fully competent to handle your own affairs, you may wish to hand over the current management of your finances or other affairs to an agent — perhaps because the agent is more skilled in those matters or you are too busy and want to be relieved of the responsibility.

You might also want to consider a power of attorney for health care. If you are seriously ill or injured, you may want someone to take the responsibility of making medical decisions for you. Your wishes concerning the kind of treatment you would prefer or refuse can be stated in a durable power of attorney for health care. If a decision is necessary, it can be made by the agent you appoint — not by a stranger in a hospital.

This kind of power of attorney can help eliminate stress, indecision, and disagreements among family members and those providing health care. It may also eliminate the need for a court petition to direct treatment or appoint an agent to act on your behalf.

For any type of power of attorney, you are advised to seek legal advice as there are different requirements in each state.

2. Why have a will?

If you fail to leave a will when you die, you make a serious and costly mistake. More than half the Americans who died last year left no will. Most people don't make a will until someone close to them dies without one. Only then, when they see the extra problems and expense caused by this omission, do they realize its importance and have one drawn up.

It is very important for both partners to have up-to-date wills. Make sure that your will reflects your current wishes about the disposal of your estate. If your disposable assets, family responsibilities (including a divorce or remarriage), or preferences change, your will must be changed as well.

Many people dislike this task, but don't let that stop you. Making a will is easy, takes very little time, effort, or expense and, when completed, the will can be filed away until needed or until changing circumstances require a revision. It is the *only* way you can be sure that after you have gone your wishes and responsibilities will be taken care of efficiently and by executors of your choice at a known cost.

The cost of state-directed disposal of your property is often more expensive than the normal procedure with a will. If there is no will, a court appoints an executor to divide the assets according to state law. This may be very different from what you would like. A substantial part could go to children and relatives, and only the remainder to your spouse, for example. This could prevent your spouse from continuing to live at the income level expected.

3. Your will

Your will should dispose of your assets in the manner you choose and to the people you desire. It should be properly drawn to ensure its acceptability to the courts and to avoid litigation. It should also take into account how to keep various taxes at a legal minimum.

The requirements of a will are well established and you can make your own. It is relatively easy to draw up your own will as long as you have a guide to assist you. If you have a complex situation, such as trust arrangements and a substantial estate, you should see an attorney. Charges for estate planning and will drafting are in the range of $75 to $150 an hour, but the money is well spent for the peace of mind it gives you.

If you die without a will, a court in the state in which you reside will appoint someone to go through the process of listing the assets and liabilities of your estate, then pay the bills and distribute the remainder to beneficiaries as prescribed by state law. While state laws differ, in general, a surviving spouse will receive about one-third to one-half of the estate with the balance divided among any living children. This arrangement may be different from what you would wish, which is why you should make a will. You have the right to make a will directing how you wish your estate to be divided and who the beneficiaries will be. A valid will may reduce court and administration costs, potential taxes, and greatly speed up and facilitate probate (i.e., the distribution of your assets).

4. The living will

For those who are concerned with the quality of life when near death, the "living will" may be the answer. A living will is a document that you draw up before you become terminally ill or incapable of stating your wishes. It is, in essence, a declaration of your intentions to the people most likely to have an influence over your care. For example, if you don't want "heroic" medical measures to be practiced on you in order to keep you alive, or to be maintained by mechanical means, you can state this in a living will. A living will can also relieve your family of the responsibility of making a very difficult decision.

Most states have laws concerning living wills and some have a particular form that must be adhered to. If you decide to draw up a living will, see an attorney to ensure that you adhere to the state regulations, then give a copy to your family physician and a close family relative.

b. FUNERAL PLANS — THE UNPOPULAR TOPIC

It is wise to make decisions about your funeral long before you expect to die. Doing so won't make any difference to you, but it certainly will to your survivors because then they will be spared this problem at a difficult time. Your death will be a shock to your spouse and family, and any assistance you can render by making advance preparations will be valuable and appreciated.

This is best done when time is available to consider the alternatives and a decision can be made on a logical, rather than emotional basis.

The following is a partial list of decisions to be made. Complete as many as you wish, but always remember to advise those who are likely to be responsible for their implementation about your decisions.

(a) If you wish, talk with a funeral director or get details from a memorial society, and have your next-of-kin with you. Most funeral directors will be happy to discuss arrangements and costs and they can also give good advice on things such as whether the service should be public or private, whether friends should be given the opportunity to visit, or whether it should be strictly a family burial with a notice after the event that it has taken place. An experienced director can tell you what others have found satisfactory and what they have found to be serious mistakes.

(b) Acquaint your family with your wishes for the actual service, but consider the beliefs and wishes of your spouse as well. He or she will want to feel included in this last act for you. A funeral that leaves your family satisfied can be important for helping them adjust to the loss. Also remember that if you plan for something that is not to the liking of your family, the final arrangements can be changed by your next-of-kin at the time of your death.

(c) Decide if you wish cremation or burial. If you want to be cremated, how should the ashes be disposed of? If you choose burial, where will it be? Now is the time to find out if there is room in a family plot or, if you need to make arrangements, to look around, compare costs, and pay for one. Prices may vary for a plot in a churchyard, in a publicly operated non-profit cemetery, or in one operated by a private organization.

(d) The final step is making the actual arrangements with the funeral director. The best way to avoid complaints about the cost of funerals is to make suitable arrangements in advance. Some directors will accept prepayment of many expenses.

c. THINK OF YOUR SPOUSE!

When making your will, changing life insurance, or purchasing an annuity or pension plan, be sure to consider your spouse's position if he or she survives you. Often this is not considered and bequests are made to children or a charity without realizing the hardship put on the surviving spouse. Therefore, you should take into account the expenses and the changes that will occur after you die and be certain to provide in full for your spouse first, unless you have made a decision to the contrary with full knowledge of what you are doing.

If you wish to make bequests to others, you can do so by a trust with a life interest to your spouse. Alternatively, both partners can make their wills at the same time and word them to reflect their joint wishes so that the desired distribution will be achieved after the second has passed away, regardless of which one goes first.

In either case, if so willed, the surviving spouse has the assets or full income for life and bequests are left to others after this obligation has been fulfilled.

1. The cost of dying

The expenses at the time of death are the funeral costs and probate and executor's fees. Funerals cost from $1,000 to $5,000, depending on how elaborate the arrangements are. Attorney's fees for probate average about 2% of the gross value of the estate. Finally, executors, unless they are also beneficiaries, will receive 2% to 4% of the gross value of the estate. There also may be outstanding debts to pay.

If the surviving spouse requires all available income, it may be unfair to divide it among others. If there is no life insurance, the money for final expenses must be drawn from savings and investments, and that will reduce your spouse's income accordingly.

2. Estate tax planning

There are no estate taxes if the value of your estate (i.e., total assets minus liabilities) is less than $600,000. There are also no estate taxes if all your assets are left to a surviving spouse even if your estate is valued at over $600,000. Estate planning is a must, however, if your estate or the combined estate of a husband and wife exceeds that $600,000 ceiling.

The first order of business in determining one's estate is producing an inventory of assets subject to estate taxes called the gross estate. Deducted from the gross estate are the expenses of the estate including the deceased person's debts, charitable bequests, and the expenses of administering the estate. Table #3 lists property subject to estate taxes.

Once the taxable estate is determined (gross estate minus deductions) the Unified Gift and Estate Tax rates are applied. Your estate tax liability is tied to any gifts you may have made. You are allowed to give away up to $10,000 per person per year without incurring a gift tax. Once you exceed that amount, you must pay a gift tax. The $600,000 exemption may be used toward your gift tax liability which reduces the exempt amount available for estate tax purposes.

TABLE #3
PROPERTY SUBJECT TO ESTATE TAXES

Real and personal property, tangible or intangible

Gift taxes paid on owing gifts made within three years of the deceased person's death

Life estates held by the deceased person

Joint interests

Transfers effective upon deceased person's death

Revocable transfers

Annuities

Joint interests

Insurance on deceased person's life

The minimum estate tax rate is 37% with a maximum rate of 55% for taxable estates over $3 million. In addition to the $600,000 exemption and unlimited marital deduction, your estate is entitled to a credit for state death taxes paid.

3. Leaving property to your spouse

Because of the unlimited marital deduction, it is advised that you use it wisely in your estate planning. You can leave at least $600,000 to someone other than your spouse and the balance of your estate to your spouse and escape estate taxes completely. However, what happens when your spouse dies? Will all those assets be taxed at that time?

One estate tax strategy may be to bequeath appreciated property to someone other than your spouse. This appreciated property is then removed from the surviving spouse's estate. And, since it gets a value at the time of your death (stepped-up basis), it can be sold with little or no income tax consequences.

Consider a trust of the $600,000 exempt from estate taxes. As long as the trust is properly drafted, you can leave the income from that trust to your spouse without having the trust included in his or her estate.

Your estate planning should also consider giving the maximum $10,000 annually to your heirs. A couple can give away $20,000 per year to any person without incurring gift taxes. This gift plan will remove assets from your estate to minimize your estate taxes.

4. Joint tenancy

While holding property by joint tenancy eliminates probate and allows the property to pass smoothly to the survivor, the tax consequences may not be what you desire. Only one half (the decedent's half) will receive a step-up in basis. Thus, if the surviving owner sells the property, a taxable gain will result.

For example, Max and Jane Giles purchased $1,000 in stock as joint tenants with the right of survivorship. The stock is worth $100,000 at the time of Max's death. One-half of the stock is now worth $50,000 and Jane's half is still worth $500. Thus, if Jane sells the stock, she would be taxed on $49,500 of gain. Had Max owned all the stock at his death, Jane would not have to pay any income tax upon selling the stock at the fair market value.

5. Private or industrial pension plans

Find out exactly what your survivors are entitled to if you are enrolled in a pension plan. There are many variations and it is very possible that, on the pensioner's death, there will be a basic reduction or complete cessation of the payments to the survivor.

If you die before receiving your pension, your beneficiaries of those pension funds may be entitled to an exclusion from income taxes of the first $5,000 they receive. In compiling your legal matters, it is advisable that you make a note of this tax benefit and attach it with other pension information.

6. Life insurance

So far, we have considered incomes that will be reduced by death. The major common source of a new flow of income is life insurance — this was the original reason for its purchase. There are many alternatives that could be selected instead of awaiting payment at death. Check them out. For example, some enable you to retain the life insurance while using its cash surrender value to produce income and eliminate the cost of carrying it.

Your final decision on the disposition of this insurance may now be determined more clearly after you have gone through the exercise of looking into the future position of your spouse after you die. You may direct in your will what is to be done with the proceeds, or you may simply make the policy payable to the beneficiary.

This step makes the proceeds payable directly to the beneficiary and while for tax purposes it is considered part of your estate, it is no longer under the control of the executor; the beneficiary has full use of it and can spend or invest it as desired.

7. Remarriage

Remarriage should be discussed long before one of the partners dies. The terms of each spouse's will may have an effect on the benefits the surviving spouse is entitled to if he or she remarries and so may affect the surviving partner's happiness seriously.

Try to think of your spouse's position, and eliminate as much emotion and jealousy as humanly possible. The survivor will be left alone at a time when your children will have their own family affairs to concern them. There are few instances where the parents live successfully with their grown children. Friends are becoming more restricted in their activities and are passing on. Single men and women are not often included in plans with couples.

Loneliness is a major problem and the support of a partner is needed more than ever. Remarriage at this stage seems to be most frequently contracted between old friends who already know each other well. Such a union brings additional financial strength because of the pooled income and brings companionship and the prospect of a few more happy years.

Frequently, widows or widowers hold back on remarriage thinking, "I wish I knew what my late spouse would think about it." This can be settled if you and your spouse discuss the issue now.

Remember that if your will is left as a trust with income to the survivor, it frequently stipulates that income ceases on remarriage. Such a provision is often put in without proper consideration. If you and your partner worked together to build your estate, is the survivor entitled to continuance of it if he or she remarries? Let your decision on this matter be one that is well thought out and mutually understood and accepted by both partners.

14
CHOOSING YOUR RETIREMENT HOME

a. WHAT SHOULD IT PROVIDE?

At each stage of your life, housing has a different function to perform. Its kind, size, and location are determined by the necessities of the various stages of life. If you had children, their welfare was probably the dominant factor when they were young. Schooling and safety of access to it, availability of playmates and recreation areas, and freedom from undesirable influences may have been decisive. Most of these factors have no value and are perhaps even disadvantages after retirement.

The design of your present home may not lend itself to retirement living, and it may require too much physical effort or expensive maintenance. Any extra room, which is no longer used, is expensive to carry in terms of taxes, heat, and upkeep. The money it is worth is tied up unproductively instead of producing income for you. Unless these costs can be offset by renting the extra space out, taking in boarders, or "duplexing," you have sufficient reason to think about moving.

The primary function of a house is the provision of shelter; your home is the place in which you eat, sleep, keep your clothes and slippers and which you use as a base — in short, where you "live." For many, their homes are merely nighttime shelters for they spend much of their day away at outside interests. To others the home provides all, or almost all, of their activities, and they spend most of their days there, going out infrequently. They are home-centered and spend little time or money elsewhere. Their homes take the place of other people's clubs and outside pursuits.

The next important factor is location. It should be near the places you frequent. If it is convenient to shopping areas, church, the library, and other places of interest, transportation will not be a problem. If it is a problem, you may not make the effort. If it is convenient for friends and relatives to come, they may drop in frequently, but if difficult, they may avoid doing so. If inconvenient, merchants may not deliver and service people might refuse to come. Obviously, location can place you either in an isolated situation and result in the loss of much that is valuable, or in the midst of those things that are important to you, therefore facilitating your enjoyment of them.

Retirement brings the need to replace the time spent at employment with new interests and perhaps changes to cope with a reduced income. It may be time to give up physically demanding work. Easily available health care assistance may be advisable. There may be a need to find new friends. The home you choose may well be the most important factor in making adjustments and determining the quality of life. Your present home may be quite satisfactory, but it is time to consider alternatives. There are many options specially conceived to provide all these conveniences for retired persons.

Many who have been living in a house find the advantages of an apartment or some form of retirement community desirable or necessary. Convenience, new friends, and new facilities may come with a multiple dwelling unit or retirement community, but new restrictions may also be introduced. Talk with people living in any new place that you may be considering. Most people will tell you about advantages and the problems. And then, if you decide to live there, you will already know your neighbors.

There is also the cost factor. It might be easier for you to rent or to buy something else. Consider all the factors discussed in this and the following chapter.

b. WHAT SHOULD IT COST?

A common question is "What percentage of our income should be spent on housing?" There is no figure that applies to everyone; each person's situation should be considered individually. It is a good question, but the decision should not be based on cost alone, for the home chosen may affect many aspects of life and often determines the success of adjustment to retirement.

When you consider how much you are going to spend on a new home, you need to total the price of the house as well as transportation and entertainment costs, for they affect each other and cannot be treated independently. This means that the money available for each of these three items should be pooled and divided to provide the most enjoyable life for you and your spouse.

Transportation can be very expensive and its cost may be an important consideration. A location that permits you to walk to most places is least expensive; public transportation is next. Lengthy automobile trips can be costly and their expense may be greater than the saving made by locating in an inexpensive but inconvenient place.

c. EVALUATING A RETIREMENT HOME

Use the following checklist to evaluate your present home for your retirement living needs and to evaluate alternatives when making a decision about whether or not to move.

(a) Does it provide the space desired?

(b) Are the facilities and fixtures suitable?

(c) Are the costs acceptable?

(d) Will its location enable you to enjoy your hobbies?

(e) Is maintenance simple and not too strenuous for you?

(f) Will your furniture fit?

(g) Is it in good repair?

(h) Will redecorating be required?

(i) Is it safe or are there hazardous features?

(j) Will you be able to leave to travel?

(k) Are pets allowed, if you have one?

(l) Are shopping, health care facilities, churches, libraries, and recreational facilities available nearby?

(m) Is it accessible to both family and friends?

(n) What will transportation costs be?

(o) Is public transportation available at the required hours?

(p) Are power, water, and sewers readily available and can fire insurance and a reasonable mortgage be obtained?

(q) Will you and your spouse really enjoy living there?

(r) Will the home be suitable for the rest of your life, or will you be faced with another move?

d. MAKING THE CHOICE

Your present home may be your best choice, but if you decide that a move may be desirable, think about what you would like to have, can afford, and if you should rent or purchase. This will also narrow the choice to areas that will meet your needs and eliminate others that definitely do not.

Be prepared to spend some time in finding the home that meets your requirements. Better to spend a few months more in the search than many unhappy years later!

1. Renting

Renting does not require money for the initial purchase and it fixes basic costs. In some cases, renting will relieve you of care and maintenance. Before you rent, check the terms of the lease carefully, as you are accepting a liability that will run for some time and cannot be changed by you without the lessor's consent. If you are not familiar with leases, it is worth having an attorney review it.

Then look at the condition of the premises and find out who will pay for any repairs and redecorating desired. This should be understood and expressed in writing. Will all your furniture fit and be satisfactory? Changes could be costly.

Before signing the lease, talk to some of the tenants and the officers of the tenants' association if there is one. You will soon learn if there are problems with the landlord or other residents that you would want to avoid.

2. Purchasing

If your decision is to purchase, there are different considerations. (If you are purchasing a condominium, see the next section.) You will be responsible for all expenses once you own the home, so the first step is to arrange for an attorney to review the offer to purchase before you sign it. A lawyer's function is to see that your interests are properly protected, that all taxes and prepaid or accrued expenses are properly apportioned, and then to search the title to be sure that you get clear ownership when you pay for it.

Once the home is yours, you are fully responsible for all repairs, maintenance, upkeep, taxes, etc., so you must investigate its condition carefully before offering to buy. An offer is understood to be for purchase in its present condition unless it states that the seller agrees to do certain things, perhaps repairs or replacements.

If the seller accepts such an offer, the repairs are then his or her responsibility, but you must be sure to have them written into the offer. In the case of a new, incomplete building, promises may be made that certain things will be done. Under no circumstances accept a verbal promise; have it clearly stated in the offer and retain a cash holdback (i.e., don't pay the full price, hold back a part) until these are completed. Insist on a larger holdback than the value of the work because this is often the only way to assure its prompt completion.

When purchasing a resale home, you are responsible for determining the condition of the property. There may be major expenses coming up. If you are competent to make the appraisal, do so; if not, get help. If you have a friend who understands construction and household equipment, this may do. You may prefer to hire a professional appraiser who will examine the building from basement to roof, advise if repairs and replacements are necessary now or will be in the near future, and estimate the cost.

Ask for verification of the operating costs, such as taxes and fuel, of the property. If there is a mortgage, ask to see it. Information supplied by agents may not be accurate. They list many properties and have been known to confuse the facts.

A piece of real estate is worth what someone will give for it today. Market conditions may change rapidly so the value may be different tomorrow. Realize that a real estate agent has been hired by the owner, not by you. Most try to be fair, but a person can't serve two masters, so do not rely on the agent to be your advisor.

Your first move is to decide what the place is worth. You can have an appraiser help you determine the value or you can compare the property to others in the same neighborhood. The Society of Real Estate Appraisers publishes a directory listing the members' names:

Society of Real Estate Appraisers
225 N. Michigan Avenue
Suite 724
Chicago, Illinois 60601
Toll-free number: 1-800-331-7732

Homes rarely sell for exactly the asking price; some asking prices are too high, some are below the actual value. If the market is rising rapidly and demand is strong, some properties bring more than the asking price as two or more purchasers bid each other up. Others take longer to sell while the owners realize what their properties are worth and finally accept the offered price. Decide what you are willing to pay, then discuss with the seller (agent) the possibility of putting in an offer lower than the asking price. The agent is obligated to take your offer to the owner who may accept or reject it, or perhaps send it back offering a compromise.

e. CONDOMINIUMS

Condominium ownership is a legal device to make it possible to purchase, rather than rent, one part of a multiple-dwelling property. The whole property is divided into self-contained living areas that are privately owned and other sections that are owned by all the owners in common. Each property must have a legal document that sets forth this division in detail, and all vary to a degree. For example, some units include the exterior building walls in the private area, others do not. This makes a difference, for if the exterior of the building is private, each owner is responsible for the maintenance of it and the window cleaning in his or her own unit; if it is owned in common, the condominium corporation will be responsible.

What you buy consists of two sections — your private apartment and the right to use all other parts of the property that are used in common by all owners. The common areas consist of everything outside the private residential units and include things such as the lobbies, passageways, service equipment, recreational facilities, and so forth. A private parking space and basement storage space may or may not be included in the purchase price, or may be available at extra cost.

Usually the builder offers the units for sale as soon as the plan has been completed and construction is about to begin. The whole project remains under the builder's ownership until the required percentage of units have been sold, the building has been basically completed, and registration is permitted.

A condominium is a corporation with a charter that sets forth the details of division of private and common elements and similar details. It sets up bylaws under which it will be operated and how the board of directors will be elected by the unit owners and what and how changes in the bylaws can be made. Only after registration can a full negotiable title with a deed be obtained for the unit for which you have paid. With the deed the property can be mortgaged, sold, or rented just as any other property can, but such acts must conform to any restrictions imposed by the bylaws. Once registered, the condominium becomes a legal entity owned jointly by the owners of the individual dwelling units.

1. Operation and cost sharing

Owners are responsible for the operation and payment of a condominium. The charter specifies what percentage of the cost of operation is to be borne by each unit. It also defines what expenses will be pooled and paid for by the condominium, rather than by the individual. These often include your power, heat, water, care of common areas, and fire insurance for the entire building. This total cost is then divided and assessed to each owner according to the charter division, and is billed monthly. This is a legal obligation and if not paid can become a charge against your property. Each owner pays private costs such as telephone and maintenance of his or her private unit.

2. Purchasing

Many of the possible traps arising when purchasing a condominium are different from those related to purchasing a house. For example, it is possible to purchase a unit either while it is under construction or after completion and it may or may not be registered. There is considerable difference in each of these situations; for your protection, sign nothing before discussing it with your attorney.

In the early stages of construction, purchase must be made from written and verbal information. Brochures with artists' sketches and plans with room sizes and details of construction and finishing should be available. Be sure that there is adequate power, water, and drainage for the equipment you desire. Copies of the plan, bylaws, and estimated operating cost should be available. Each state sets the basic disclosures, guarantees, and protective measures required. Finished demonstration units may be available for inspection.

Buying a condominium at this stage can be risky. You usually must put down a deposit and agree to pay the balance when your unit is ready for occupancy, which may be before registration. The builder estimates a completion date which could be delayed by strikes, financial problems, etc. Construction could cease, leaving you in a bind. If you purchase during construction, be prepared for delays. Only purchase from a builder with good financial strength and with a reputation for finishing on time, delivering well-built units, correcting deficiencies, and accurately estimating costs.

Depending on your agreement to purchase, you may be required to pay for your unit when it is ready, even if it is not registered. If so, your monthly payments are considered as rent and you are a tenant without a deed. Your attorney can protect against problems that could arise in such circumstances.

If you purchase after completion and registration, you can inspect the unit and common areas and get the feel of the place. You can meet and talk with your neighbors and decide if you would enjoy living with them. You will learn if they are satisfied and if they propose changes. If the building has been operating for a year or more, the accuracy of the operating expenses will be known and management quality assessed. You will get a deed and an exact date for closing your purchase.

In general, if you have been living in a house or a rented apartment, there may be many differences in condominium living of which you may not be aware. These could include loss of privacy, living under majority control, inconvenient parking for you and your guests, rules about pets, garbage disposal, security problems, and elevators. Discuss such things with those experienced in condominium living; they can give valuable information.

Legislation governing condominiums comes under the jurisdiction of the states and all the bylaws must conform to their statutes.

3. **Owner's responsibilities and costs**

(a) The owner of a unit has a vote in the formation of the bylaws and must accept any responsibility or cost they impose.

(b) Each person has the usual cost of maintaining his or her own living unit in the manner in which he or she pleases.

(c) Payment for utilities may be partly common and partly private, depending on the bylaws.

(d) Separate real estate taxes are levied on each unit just as they would be on a house.

(e) If you have a mortgage on your unit, you are responsible for it.

(f) Insurance on the unit may be covered adequately and be paid for in the monthly fee, or you may elect to purchase additional insurance at your own expense.

(g) At the time of purchase, there are the expenses related to any real estate transactions, such as legal fees, adjustments, and transfer taxes.

4. **Some advantages of condominium ownership**

(a) You own your own home. This means security of tenure as there is no lease to be terminated.

(b) You can usually purchase similar space at a lower price than you would pay for a free standing house.

(c) Part of your capital may be released and is available for income-producing investment or perhaps the purchase of a summer or winter holiday home.

(d) Your money is invested in your own home.

(e) Under present laws, if it is your principal residence, there may be no federal income tax on any profit made when it is sold *if* you sell your property after reaching age 55 *or* within 2 years of selling your old home you purchase a new home of greater or equal value.

(f) Ownership will control one of the problems associated with rent. If the value of a rental unit increases, the owner usually increases the rent. You will avoid this in a condominium. Improvements you pay for increase the value of your property.

(g) Your unit can be mortgaged.

(h) You are freed of many of the responsibilities of property maintenance and operation.

(i) By electing the directors and voting on the bylaws, you participate in management and can express your wishes and protect your interests. When renting you may not be consulted when changes affecting you are being considered.

(j) The cost of major items, such as a swimming pool, is divided among all owners, and this may make available facilities that you could not afford to purchase yourself.

5. Some disadvantages of ownership

(a) You surrender some independence and become subject to majority control.

(b) Cost decisions are group decisions. As an example, you may be required to help pay for a swimming pool which you may not want or use.

(c) You have the responsibilities of ownership. If you wish to move you must arrange its sale or rental. If you rent, you walk out at the end of the lease without further property considerations.

(d) The money invested is tied up and not available, although taking a mortgage could provide the major part of the investment if desired.

(e) There may be some restrictions on sale or leasing in the bylaws.

6. What to watch for

When you are buying a condominium, you should watch for all the usual things that apply to the purchase of any home. But there are special problems that apply only to condominiums.

First, if the development has not been completed and turned over by the developer to the owners, you are simply renting from the developer. Any payments on the unit may be considered as rent until the turnover takes place. You may have serious problems if the development takes a long time to complete or goes bankrupt.

Second, when you are purchasing at this stage, the statements of expected monthly operating costs are just estimates and may be misleading, so you should compare these estimates with actual costs for similar properties.

Third, the bylaws set up for the development period will be subject to review and possible change when the owners take over. Try to meet some of the present occupants and ask if they are happy or would like to see changes.

Fourth, you should obtain a copy of the declaration and bylaws, read them, and have an attorney familiar with condominium law review and explain them to you.

f. COOPERATIVE APARTMENTS

A cooperative apartment is different from a condominium in that the cooperative owns all the property and you buy shares from it and rent your unit from it. You become responsible for the expense of the cooperative through the obligation attached to the ownership of these shares. You remain responsible until your shares have been sold and transferred to another owner, and you do not have a deed but a proprietary lease.

Any mortgage is on the whole property and you have no choice but to bear your share. You may become responsible for bearing a large part of the cost of carrying vacant space, should vacancies occur. In a condominium, these costs would accrue against the owner of the vacant units and would be recovered on sale, provided the price is high enough to yield an adequate surplus.

The organization is run by a board of directors elected by the leaseholders. The bylaws specify the rights and obligations of the tenants and any prohibitions. For example, subletting or taking in boarders may be prohibited.

Cooperatives are usually required to carry insurance on all co-op owned property, but you may require additional personal insurance. The directors must provide an annual statement showing interest or other payments made on your behalf that may be required for your income tax preparation.

If you contemplate purchasing shares in a cooperative apartment, be sure to understand all the obligations and implications before signing anything. The laws concerning cooperatives differ from state to state, so you may want to consult an attorney experienced in this area of the law.

g. RENTAL APARTMENTS

The alternatives can be narrowed down if your financial situation favors rented rather than owned premises. Renting frees your capital for income production. The rental charged for such a suite may be lower than the cost of carrying the comparable living space in a house.

For the retired person, there are a great many advantages to renting an apartment. Some rental buildings cater to young families, and some to older people without families. This can be important. (One person who lives in an apartment building occupied by her contemporaries reports that she can enjoy a card game every night with neighbors, without ever leaving the building!)

There is no physical effort required in caring for the lawn or building or removing snow. The cost is known, which is important to anyone on a tight budget, and if you travel for a time, things will be looked after during your absence.

h. MOBILE OR MANUFACTURED HOMES

1. What are they like?

Just what is a mobile home? If you have not been in a modern mobile home (now often called a manufactured home), you may be very agreeably surprised when you see one.

The increase in the sale of mobile homes for use as permanent dwellings has been rapid. If you visit dealerships where mobile homes are sold, it will soon become apparent that retired couples are buying many of them.

There are two types of mobile units which are frequently confused. The trailer or RV provides temporary, compact accommodation that can be taken along as you travel. The "mobile home" is similar in exterior appearance to a trailer but is much larger. In spite of the name, it is not really mobile in the same sense as the trailer. It is usually much too large to be towed by an ordinary automobile and is not equipped with its own wheels. It is taken on a large truck to a location where it is set up on a permanent foundation. (It is now common to build a basement and place this "mobile" on top.) In reality, mobile homes are factory-built homes, designed so they can be transported as units then set up on permanent foundations and left there the same as any other house.

Regular "parks" provide sewers, water, and electricity which are permanently connected. The unit is mobile when compared to a standard house only in that it can be picked up from the foundation and moved to a new location if and when desired.

Mobile homes are meant to be permanent dwellings. They are well-designed and durable and many are built by established, reputable companies. They come in either single or double widths. The singles are about 12 to 14 feet wide and frequently as long as 60 feet. The doubles are built in two sections, divided down the middle so that the two halves, when assembled side by side, make up dwellings that are approximately twice as wide as the single units. They must be built in this manner so that they can be transported by road in the usual way and joined together on the site making it possible to have a home as large as 28' x 60', which permits wider rooms and a center hall. They are often spacious and may have a living room, a dining room, den, one to three bedrooms, kitchen, utility room, and bathroom.

If they are placed on a regular basement, a workshop and storage space can help keep the floor warmer in winter. A canopy to cover a patio is common.

Appliances are usually modern and smart. The bathroom may have modern fixtures, a built-in vanity and counter-top, and mirrors and exhaust fans. Size and space is little problem unless you are looking for unusually large rooms. Equipment may include a freezer, refrigerator, electric or gas stove, double stainless steel sink, and built-in cupboards and counters. Each model is usually offered in an assortment of interior decorator designed color schemes. Some even have woodburning fireplaces.

When you purchase a standard house, the lot is part of the package. But, in the case of mobiles, the location on which to place it is usually a separate deal (although some parks do provide the site and home together). You should not purchase the home until you have selected and obtained the site, possibly the most difficult part. You are not free to park the unit on any available land that can be purchased or rented because there are often land use restrictions.

2. Choosing the location

Be careful when choosing the location for a mobile home for it will contribute to the quality of life. Many parks and communities are well planned, organized, and fun, but others are not. In some, the homes are crowded together and in others there is plenty of room for a garden and outdoor living.

Be sure there is adequate water, sewage, and electricity and that financial and insurance companies regard the site favorably. Assess the convenience of the location: is it close to shopping, libraries, churches, and restaurants? Does the park offer organized activities such as exercise classes or hobby classes? People are happiest when living among people of similar backgrounds and interests. Look for a location where the residents are like yourself.

Obtaining a suitable location on which to place the home may be difficult. Some parks may insist that you buy the home through them, which is fine if their prices are competitive. This arrangement has the advantage of assuring that a standard will be maintained thus protecting your investment.

Some parks sell the lots and charge a monthly fee to pay for the services provided. Others rent or lease the lots and charge a comparatively higher monthly fee. If your intended location is not in an established park, be sure that the local bylaws will permit its use for your plan. One of the great drawbacks is the shortage of suitable lots, and one you will enjoy may be difficult to find. Obtain copies of all rules and regulations to which any site is subject.

Most regulatory bylaws are made by, and are under the control of, the state and the local municipality. There is little uniformity. In some rural areas, there are practically no restrictions; in others, mobile homes are treated the same as conventional structures and must conform to the land-use bylaws. In other places, municipalities have permitted separate sites to be set aside and used for mobile homes with specific provisions for them. Some sites are on the outskirts of towns and use all the town's amenities. Others are set up as independent communities with facilities of their own.

3. Financing

A mortgage may be available when the home is located in some well-run parks, otherwise financing is usually done on the same basis as automobiles, which means a high rate of interest. If you are borrowing on other security through a bank, a lower rate may be possible. Financing is often done through the dealer and may include furnishings, delivery, and setting up the home. In some cases, units can be financed with Veteran Administration and Federal Housing Act loans. Mobile homes purchased with the land may receive financing of up to 30 years, thereby reducing your monthly payments.

4. What to watch for

When buying a mobile home, remember that all are not of the same quality and some will give less trouble and be better than others. Appraise the quality of materials and construction of the various makes. Consider purchasing from an established reputable dealer only, for he or she is less likely to handle an inferior product. The dealer's experience can also be valuable in assisting you with the selection of the most suitable model and options for you.

Some mobile homes are fire hazards, containing too many flammable materials, or are poorly designed so that a fire once started is difficult to contain. Another complaint is unsafe design; there are insufficient escape points and occupants could be trapped. These factors have resulted in high insurance rates and in some cases insurance cannot be purchased at all. Before buying the home or contracting for the lot, contact your insurance agent to be sure insurance is available and what it will cost.

All mobile homes built since 1976 for use in the United States must meet the construction, durability, and safety standards set by the Department of Housing and Urban Development (HUD). A HUD-approved mobile home will display a red and silver metal plate placed on the outside of it. In addition to the HUD seal, manufacturers and retailers are often required to provide warranties on the mobile home's safety and provide remedies for defects. Such warranties are often enforceable under federal law and some state laws.

The dealer is responsible for arranging delivery and is the first contact for the correction of any repairs or deficiencies under the warranty; if the dealer is cooperative, the inevitable problems will be readily corrected. Examine the warranty carefully and compare those offered by various makers.

Before purchasing the home or signing up for a location, see your attorney and ask him or her to review the contract and warranty for the home and the terms involved in renting the lot. There may be many things you do not understand or may not have asked, and an experienced attorney will spot them quickly.

i. THE RETIREMENT COMMUNITY

Retirement communities can add a whole new dimension to life for their residents. These communities offer a greater opportunity for an active and interesting lifestyle than could be easily found elsewhere. They are a combination of homes and amenities specifically suited to retirees and there is a wide range in quality and cost.

The living quarters in retirement communities are usually mobile homes or apartments. Some offer swimming pools, tennis and shuffleboard courts, even lakes and golf courses. Others may employ an activities organizer to arrange card games, dances, parties, and social activities. Some have shopping centers, restaurants, and laundry facilities. Medical services may also be provided.

j. WHEN MORE HELP IS REQUIRED

Specialists in the field agree that it is best for older people to carry on in their own homes if possible. It is recognized that they will retain their abilities longer if they use them on their own behalf, and any special provisions should be made only for those who require it. Support services may provide all that is needed. The degree and kind of assistance required will vary from person to person, and there is a wide range of choices to suit all needs.

Often individuals have moved into nursing homes because they required certain care that had to be provided by trained professionals, and these were the only places where such care was available. Now many municipalities provide and pay for the health support service such as a visiting nurse, therapist, homemaker, or others, if by so doing the person can remain independent. Ask about these services through your doctor or the local public health nurse who will know what services are available and how best they can be provided.

1. **Retirement homes**

There is a wide range of retirement homes available for consideration. Some are organized simply to provide easier, more secure independent living. There are also graduated degrees of assistance available in others. A common type is one step removed from regular apartments. Tenants often have one large room per person or couple with a private bathroom, cupboard space, etc. They may use some of their own furniture, pictures, and ornaments, which enables them to bring a few of the familiar mementos of their lives with them. There may be a common room with television and a dining room where meals are served. Breakfast may be delivered to each room. Nursing and medical services may be available and are often included in the price. This may be an important comfort. Anyone can come and go without any constraint just as you would in a regular apartment.

As loneliness is one of the difficult problems of older persons, these homes provide an answer because you live with a group that can provide instant companionship. There are usually activities such as bingo, cards, and dances available. Such residences have been happy homes for many who have no handicap and don't need the extra facilities but enjoy living in this atmosphere. Others with some physical or medical disability find the provision for health care a very helpful form of security.

Retirement homes are not the answer for everyone. Someone who must have a garden or a basement workshop, and the person who makes his or her own opportunities may not be happy in a communal setting. The "loner," who just can't stand crowds and does not enjoy group activities, probably will not fit in. Too often those responsible for the welfare of an older relative know of one person who is happy in such a residence and accept this as the answer for their relative. But if the relative has a personality unsuited for this life, a retirement home may be the worst choice.

Beyond the apartment described above, alternatives range from places where only slightly more care is given, up to those where patients receive what is equivalent to full invalid's bed care.

If you have some disability, a move to a retirement home may be very desirable and comforting. If you have a health problem, there may be very little alternative. Proper care may be essential. This is a matter to discuss and decide with your physician.

An older person, living alone, particularly if he or she has mobility or health problems, may lose interest in food, find difficulty in participating in activities with others, and become a recluse. This may contribute to mental and physical deterioration. Such an individual may benefit greatly from proper diet and health care. It may lead to a better attitude and improvement of retention of mental faculties because of the participation in a more normal and interesting social life.

2. Choosing the home

If you are making a choice for yourself, or are finding a home for a relative, by all means investigate any place you are considering. Go personally, talk to the residents, go through the building, try and see the meals being served. Be critical and careful for not all have proper standards of care and treatment of their residents.

The most important feature of any retirement home may be the attitude of the staff to the residents. Many who work in the field think that mental activity is retained and the symptoms of aging delayed if the residents are treated with respect as responsible adults and encouraged to make decisions rather than ordered around like children. A person treated as incapable comes to accept the fact that this is so, and many who are considered senile are not.

A convenient location that your friends and relatives can easily visit, and from which transportation is available to shopping and other places of interest is an advantage. A choice of suitable activities will make for pleasant days, and it is in this area that great strides are being made. It is increasingly recognized that providing proper food, shelter, and medical care is not enough. Participation with others is not only a source of happiness but also contributes greatly to the maintenance of health. The better homes now have extensive internal programs and also arrange group trips out to shop, visit the country, or do other interesting things. This helps you retain the feeling of being a part of the world rather than being shut off from it.

3. The life care retirement community

A life care retirement community is a relatively new concept in retirement housing. The idea is that you can move into the community at any stage of retirement — at any stage of independent living — and stay there for the rest of your life regardless of how little or much medical assistance you may need. Recreational facilities and social activities are available for you if you are completely independent but want the added security of the community; but if you become more dependent on other people and medical assistance you can stay in your home and get the help you need.

There are now about 700 life care communities in the United States. Each has its own concept, program, price level, and rules. In most, the residents must buy an apartment with a buy back agreement that sets the basis of repurchase that may be an annually decreasing price until a specified level is reached from which it drops no further. In addition, there may be a substantial cash endowment payment required, and there may be a monthly fee.

These communities try to offer residents a full, active, interesting, secure life among friends for the remainder of their days, at a known cost. If disability or serious illness occurs, assistance is immediately available so they can remain in familiar surroundings rather than be forced into a strange institution.

The decision to move into a life care community may require a large financial commitment. To be certain the organization is well managed and able to live up to its obligations, ask a financially trained person to investigate the financial condition of the community. It is also advisable to have an attorney examine the legal documents involved so that you are sure you understand your rights and obligations.

k. CARING FOR AN ELDERLY RELATIVE OR SPOUSE

During your retirement, you may be responsible for a parent or spouse who reaches the stage where he or she cannot continue to live independently. There is danger of accident, deteriorating health from lack of care, and malnutrition from improper eating habits. A person in this state may turn inward as it becomes more difficult to go out and participate. These factors together with loneliness and fear lead to unhappiness which may further accelerate the decline.

The elderly often persist in continuing in this sorry state rather than risking the unknowns of change. But although a change may not be ideal, it would surely be an improvement. What should be done? It is difficult to force the move against a loved one's wishes, but it may be the greatest kindness.

If the move can be made into some family setting acceptable to all concerned, that might be the best solution. People at this stage become almost childlike in their dependence on others and it is a comfort to be with relatives. Life has little to offer, there is no future, and the family to which they devoted much of their lives and which they helped to create is the one remaining thing which they hold dear. However, this option is not always possible either for lack of space or because such a move might place too great a strain on the household.

If you decide that your relative must enter a home, the first step is for you to investigate those homes available locally. Some are privately operated and are more expensive, but a range of costs may be found in your area. Public or church-supported ones may scale their costs depending on the person's financial position.

Once you have made the decision, attempt to obtain agreement on the advantages of making the move, for experience shows that the person who makes it willingly adjusts more easily to the change. It is a big dislocation to close up one's home and move into a new environment with strangers, but there are many advantages. The care that will become increasingly important is available, and the lonely life, often restricted to a room or two, is replaced with companionship and activities. These may be important factors in maintaining interest in life and mental alertness.

If you decide to move your relative into such a residence, you will probably worry about his or her happiness, and, truthfully, your relative may *not* be happy. You must expect this reaction and be prepared to cope with it. Remember, however, that he or she may be safer and more comfortable than if left in the previous difficult circumstances, and happiness may come later.

The change is great and comes at an age where it is difficult to adjust. The first period of weeks or months may be one of constant complaints and pleas to "get me out of here." But, with time, the strangeness wears off, friendships form, interests develop, and the new life often improves health and becomes more enjoyable than the old.

The greatest fear of the elderly is to be placed in a home and be forgotten; the greatest joy is an invitation to visit the family and see the grandchildren; phone calls, letters, visits and other caring contact are bright spots in their lives.

For more information on caring for an elderly relative, see *Taking Care*, another title in the Self-Counsel Series.

15
WHERE WILL YOU LIVE?

If you want to achieve as much as possible from retirement, your home should be located wherever your needs and desires are best met. You may conclude that your present home, or another in the same community, is the best choice for you. There are many advantages to staying where you are: proximity to family and friends, familiarity of the shops and amenities, and so on. The hassles and uncertainties of change are eliminated. If you can happily fill your days, there may be no reason to consider a move.

However, you may belong to the percentage of the retired population that wants or needs to move. In that case, you should consider the issues discussed in this chapter.

a. FINANCIAL CONSIDERATIONS

If you have completed your estimates of retirement income and expenses and you find no financial problems, money will have no bearing on your decision to move. However, if there is going to be insufficient income to fulfill all desires, you should now make plans to be able to live within your means.

There are a number of suggestions made in chapter 11 to assist in increasing income or cutting expenses; the most important of these are related to moving. These options might solve your financial problems and yield other benefits. You may help the situation by making a move, if you live in a large city, to a small town or less-expensive spot in the country. Often a move to a rural area brings major savings in addition to those from housing. For example, if you have been a member of a recreation club in any major center, the cost has undoubtedly been high. This expense would certainly be a consideration if you are under pressure to cut your spending. In a rural area, you can usually join golf, bingo, bridge, and any other clubs and participate in all the activities for a small fraction of their cost in the city. Clubs in a rural setting may not have as elaborate facilities as those in the city, but these may not be important to you. The difference in cost, on the other hand, may mean simply that you will be able to continue with the activity rather than being forced to discontinue it.

The adjustment to living on a lower income in a smaller center is less than moving to another country, for example. You might also find that changes in your lifestyle provoke less reaction from others than in the more rigid social strata of a larger center.

Also, it is possible to move to or near a small city or a town with excellent facilities, economical living, and outdoor activities available close to home. Thus, one place can double as a home and a holiday cabin or cottage. There are many such communities in America, for example, Chapel Hill, North Carolina; Prescott, Arizona; Clearwater, Florida; La Jolla, California — just to name a few across the country.

b. POSSIBILITY OF EMPLOYMENT

One of the important considerations of determining location is the possibility of finding a full- or part-time job. Post-retirement jobs are scarce, so if you want to have a suitable one, this will probably decide the location in which you will live. It may be easier to find work where you are or in an industrial or commercial area. Be certain of the job possibilities available in any place you plan to locate. In many "retirement communities," there are many job seekers and very few opportunities. Some areas also refuse to grant work permits to individuals until they have resided there for a reasonably lengthy qualifying period. Check out all these things first to avoid serious disappointment.

c. A BETTER CLIMATE

Climate may not be the most important factor; to many the pull back home to where there are still relatives, activities, and a lifestyle they grew to enjoy when younger, may have the stronger appeal. But for northerners wanting a change from long cold winters, the southeast and the southwest areas should be considered. Southern California is known for its sea-moderate climate. It has a short winter with no snow to speak of and little hot weather in summer. It rarely rains and certainly does not have the humidity of Florida or coastal Texas.

Florida's Gulf Coast weather is pleasing to most. Its winter temperatures average 62°F. Its humid summers with an average temperature of 86°F are tolerable because of the pleasant bay breezes that flow in after the sun sets. Local beaches in and around Sarasota, Florida are said to be the whitest and finest in the state.

For some people, the hot, humid summer of the south is just as undesirable as the colder, northern winter is for others. The ideal may be to retain the permanent home but to leave temporarily during the unpleasant months. The permanent home provides roots of friends and family and the other — perhaps rented — can give a break every year from the poor weather. Most people who move a considerable distance choose a location where friends are established. People from one city, area, or state tend to cluster together and a sizable community of people with a common background develops.

d. MOVE TO A FOREIGN COUNTRY WITH CAUTION!

One of the possibilities that retired people consider is moving to the warmer climate of a foreign country. If you make a full change of residence, you are not required to give up your American citizenship, but for tax and legal purposes you will probably be under the jurisdiction of your adopted country as well as the United States. Regardless of where you live, you must file a U.S. tax return.

According to the Social Security Administration, the top 10 foreign countries for Americans receiving social security checks in the last few years were Canada, Mexico, Italy, West Germany, Greece, the Philippines, Portugal, Ireland, Israel, and Spain. Your social security retirement checks can be delivered anywhere in the world except Albania, Cambodia, Cuba, East Germany, North Korea, and Vietnam. Secure a copy of the booklet *Your Social Security Checks While You Are Outside the United States* from your Social Security Administration office before making that move.

1. What can you gain or lose?

The obvious advantage to moving to a foreign country is usually a warmer climate, but there can be a hot or humid season that may be unpleasant. If the year-round conditions are suitable, you can enjoy a more active and enjoyable outdoor life and the selection of a suitable climate may alleviate arthritic or bronchial conditions.

Taxes and living costs may be lower in many countries. Some people hope for more economical living in a low-cost area. On the other hand, there is the problem of health care, which becomes more important with each passing year. Medicare does not provide health benefits if you live outside the United States. Are you prepared to pay more in health insurance if your present insurance carrier does not provide coverage if you live abroad? Will you accept the medical facilities, and when old age and perhaps separation from your spouse comes, will satisfactory living arrangements be available? Further, are you prepared to live under the laws of your adopted country?

2. Possible language difficulties

If you are thinking of moving to a country that uses a language you do not speak, consider the special difficulties. If you don't learn the new language, you can find yourself in a difficult position, often seriously so, if ill or in trouble.

A language you know may be spoken in certain shops or in a colony of visitors, but unless you are willing and able to learn the local language, the inability to communicate elsewhere may become troublesome and this is frequently why people who emigrate eventually return home.

3. The best of both worlds

Often, retired people decide to move permanently to another country because it is less expensive than maintaining two homes. But if you can afford to have both, the best part of each year can be spent in each. As well, you can maintain closer ties with family and friends and keep that valuable medical/hospital/retirement home connection that may soon become important to you and your spouse. Family and old friends usually mean much to retired people, and one of the common reasons for coming back given by those who moved away is that they just missed them too much and nothing else took their place. Families cannot be replaced by new ones in another location and good friendships take years to develop.

e. DIFFERENT VIEWS OF MOVING

Often, spouses have very different views about moving to another country at retirement. If one of you has been working and the other staying at home for a number of years, the changes inherent in retirement are very different for each. The person retiring now has his or her whole day to replan and loses many things of value, such as the companionship of a work group. It can be very helpful to look forward to a move to some favored spot as one of the main benefits of retirement. The old associations of the job can be left behind and it will be easier to get into the new routine. A completely new list of interests will be introduced.

On the other hand, a spouse who has stayed at home over the years may not want to leave the household routine and activities that are neighborhood-oriented; moving may mean complete loss. Moving away may be a greater adjustment for a homemaker who has made the home reflect a personal lifestyle.

For these reasons, considerable compromise between the spouses may be necessary. Understanding and cooperation may be required to maintain harmony in the marriage.

f. TRY IT OUT FIRST!

Don't move to some distant point with which you are not really familiar or that you know only through the descriptions of friends or from a short holiday in the region. Living permanently somewhere is much different from vacationing there. If you move there, you will be staying in a different place, doing different things, and the glamour that comes with a holiday soon wears off.

What will it be like when you must spend year after year there? Look at all aspects carefully. Can you afford it? Are there activities you require, not only to use your time pleasantly but to provide those psychological satisfactions you require? What about health care? Is the climate, on a year-round basis, acceptable? If you have friends and family that mean much to you, will you be able to see them often enough?

There is only one way to answer these questions to your satisfaction, and that is to have a try-out before making a permanent move. You should actually live there for as long as possible before making the step a definite one. Rent the kind of living accommodation you plan to use. Move in as a permanent resident, not a tourist, and live as you plan to live. Try out the activities in which you plan to participate. Meet the people you will have to live with once you are there.

Will you enjoy living with them? Stay on through the most unpleasant period of the year. Stay long enough for the novelty to wear off and the problems to develop. Rent out your present home for perhaps six months or a year. Any difference in cost will be well worth it, and will be much less than the cost of selling, relocating, and then doing it all over again if the move turns out to be undesirable. Consider each factor, think of the arguments in favor and against moving. If, after you have done the homework and you and your spouse both agree to go, do it and good luck!

16

YOUR HEALTH AND RETIREMENT
by Paul D. Clarke, M.D.

For most of us, the magic number "65" has been held up as the finishing line. Compulsory retirement, pension plan, social security, "Goodbye and Good Luck!"

Happily, society is re-examining this arbitrary cut-off age. Why someone doing a good job at age 64.9 years is thought to be incapable a few weeks later is beyond me. Winston Churchill started in office in May, 1940, a few weeks after his sixty-fifth birthday. I know a medical person who was "retired" by the University Teaching Hospital; he spent the next three years in Africa teaching, practicing, and running a new medical school. Anyone at 65 who is healthy and active should have the right to work.

The pessimists say that in this inflationary age with the eroding value of pension plans, we will all have to stay in harness forever.

Despite these diverse factors, 65 is still retirement age for the next few years. It is important to realize that despite all the changes that will occur on that day, your mind and body don't change into a retirement phase.

The progression from late middle age (55 to 65) to the "young old" age group (65 to 75) is slow and continuous. Nothing sudden and dramatic will happen, as it does from age 10 to 15. The important thing is to *preserve what you have.* The ancient Greeks taught us "that which is not used, atrophies." An active body will be firmly muscled. Two years of inactivity will cause great muscle shrinking. The same process will happen to your mind if you don't keep it "in gear" and busy.

a. FIND SOMETHING TO DO

A soldier-poet in the trenches in 1917 wrote that if he lived through Flanders, he would "sit on my ass for 50 years, then hang my hat on a pension." Anything was an improvement over the Western Front, no doubt! This "do nothing" policy is unwise for the rest of us. You should plan what you are going to *do* with yourself when you reach retirement age.

Just as you plan your financial future, you must plan for your activities. Many of you have hobbies and interests that you are looking forward to fully developing. Many will carry on working. Those who don't want to work after 65 and have not developed any leisure time pursuits are at risk.

The sudden break from a lifetime of struggle will be wonderful...for a few weeks. Then what? There are just not that many odd jobs around the house and garden to keep you "tuned up." Daytime TV is an easy way to pass the time. You can always look out the window...or listen to the radio. Two or three years of this type of voluntary inertia (a polite way of saying "hog lazy") will produce a bored and very dull person. The odds are great that depression will set in. Then you can sit and worry all day about that sore back or that headache you had last week.

A vicious circle of pain-worry-depression leading to more pain-worry-depression can be set up. Any pain or discomfort is influenced by the state of mind. This is all too common after retirement. Many times the basic cause of vague pains is not diagnosed immediately by the doctor. This leads to tests and more visits to the doctor's office. This, of course, causes more stress, more worry, and the vicious circle rolls on.

This is the background to a situation we have all heard of on occasion — death within a year or two of retirement. "Never sick a day in his life, just up and died last week."

Convinced? Please, keep busy!

b. MAINTAINING GOOD HEALTH

Having decided not to "go to seed" upon starting retirement is a major first step. The next step is to consider the rule of sensible living that our mothers taught us years ago. Today, this is called lifestyle counseling. The TV ads and the papers and magazines are full of all sorts of advice these days. You can't follow all these multimedia instructions, but you should consider making changes in your various activities and habits.

1. Exercise

A degree of physical fitness is a good thing because you feel better. Stress problems are fewer because we cope better with stress if the body is in shape. You don't have to go into Olympic training, but daily exercise is advised. The cheapest, easiest, and most readily available is a brisk 15-minute walk.

It may take a while to build up to being able to do 15 minutes of non-stop walking, but there's no hurry. The heart and lungs get a good work-out and they are the most important. Swimming is great, too, if you have access to a pool.

More vigorous exercise is fine for those who have been doing it all along. If you feel the need to jog or play tennis, see your doctor first for advice about your own unique physical capabilities.

2. Diet

Volumes are written these days about nutrition and weight loss. Many controversies exist about health foods and vitamins. "Dr. Wonderful's" latest diet to cure heart disease will be seen in all the papers next week. Much that is written is sensible. Much more is absolute bunkum.

We are in an era of concern and awareness about good nutrition. We worry about toxic fertilizers, toxic sprays on crops, and cattle dosed with medications to increase their muscle bulk. We are told to take vitamins A to Z. Lose 25 pounds or else. Drink milk, but stay away from dairy products.

For anyone who is not on a specific, prescribed diet, and just wants sensible up-to-date advice on what and how much to eat, there is one common sense rule. Whatever you do, do it slowly and sensibly and in moderation.

3. Alcohol

Our society generally accepts "social" drinking. The problem is, what is "social" drinking? If I drink only when in company, can I drink as much and as often as I want?

Doctors don't have a good definition of alcoholism. I know some teetotal M.D.s who will write "chronic alcoholism" on a patient's chart. The patient enjoys a drink or two after work and may get a bit tight at a party once a month! Other doctors define an alcoholic as "someone who drinks more than I do."

Once again, moderation is the key. Also, never use alcohol as a medicine. Don't drink to get to sleep, or to "feel better," or to "brace up" for a business or social event. Herein begins the road to alcoholism and all the dreary misery that accompanies this diagnosis.

Alcohol is socially acceptable to most of us when used to relax in good company. We all know when to say enough. Specific illnesses will preclude any alcohol, of course. Most common is an active ulcer.

Remember, medicines and alcohol do not mix! Too many deaths occur because people mix tranquilizers or pain killers with alcohol. Maybe the doctor forgot to warn them. Maybe they forgot. Maybe they thought the doctor was being a fuss-pot.

Those who take pills and alcohol together stand a very good chance of (as the Irishman said) "waking up dead in the morning."

4. Smoking

Don't smoke! It can cause lung disease; chronic bronchitis — coughing; emphysema — bad shortness of breath; lung cancer — death. It can also increase your chances of artery disease (i.e., strokes, heart attacks). These are hard, cold facts. Your mother warned you. King James I banned tobacco smoking in his court.

However, many people enjoy smoking and do not want to quit. We do not live in a rational world, and wanting to smoke is a purely emotional decision. If you are in this group, I would ask you to cut down. Some doctors are pretty tough with smokers and will discharge them from the practice if they won't quit. Personally, I think this is abandoning a patient, which I never do. (You may be a damn fool, but I'll look after you.)

If you smoke 30 cigarettes a day, ease down to 15. At least you are smoking less. You might cut down on the horrendous odds facing you. You might even convince yourself to quit altogether.

AND NOW FOLKS, FOR SOMETHING THAT OUR PARENTS PROBABLY DIDN'T TELL US ABOUT

5. Sex

Volumes are written about sex these days. Most of them seem based on techniques and ratings and read like the statistics of a world series game. The present generation really didn't invent love-making, but they are certainly much more open about it.

I think the majority of people looking at retirement planning are of an age who feel that their sex life is a private matter. In fact it is so private that they won't discuss it with their doctor. Even if they have, there is a good chance that the doctor was too ill-informed or embarrassed or shocked to offer any advice beyond "learn to live with the problem."

Sex is a pretty basic urge. It compares with hunger and thirst as far as the urge itself is concerned. Society teaches restraint from an early age, and many are reticent about discussing any sexual problem. Until recently, medical schools didn't teach doctors anything about sex therapy.

An unresolved sexual problem is a source of stress. If we can't cope with a stress we get a symptom. This might be nervousness and irritability. If we "bury" the problem, then a psychosomatic symptom will probably develop — headache, sleeplessness, ulcer, or whatever. If we don't talk about the cause, then we only get treated for the symptom. If you have a problem, tell your doctor. If the response is inadequate, ask for a referral to someone skilled in this field.

Most sexual problems are emotional in origin. In other words, they are "people" problems. If a marriage is sick, the sexual aspect of the marriage likely won't be very good either. Sex and love go together with most people. Some problems have no solution. Partners in a marriage doomed to failure likely have sexual problems that won't be resolved. If the marriage is basically sound, then problems are probably able to be helped.

Much impotence (failure to get or keep an erection) in the male is due to tension or fatigue. Sometimes it just happens. When it is an occasional event, don't worry. If it happens a lot, see your doctor. Sometimes it is a physical problem (artery disease; diabetes).

Painful intercourse (dysparevnia) in a women can be emotionally or physically determined. Medical advice is needed if this is a recurring problem.

With advancing years, the male erection may be less easily aroused and less firm. A woman's lubricant glands may be less active. These are normal, common events. Prescription: Take two people in the mood; add a little baby oil, and a little imagination.

To quote the same Irishman as before, "May you live as long as you want to, and may you want to as long as you live."

c. ENTER THE DOCTOR

After 65, medical needs begin to increase. Older people see a doctor more often than younger people. More seniors are admitted to hospital. Self-responsibility is very important in maintaining good health, but you do need to have a good doctor.

Don't wait until you need a doctor before finding one. Everyone needs a periodic checkup. Certain examinations should be carried out at regular intervals, especially as you get into late middle age. Blood pressure should be checked annually even in the most healthy. Breast and pelvic examinations are advised for women on a regular basis.

A good family doctor will coordinate your needs for checkups, and is available as a counselor on health maintenance. Even if you are disgustingly healthy, you should see a family doctor periodically. If you get sick, you then have a doctor who knows you! If you need a specialist and hospital care, you have a friend who can navigate the sometimes confusing path among several specialists in a big hospital. Your doctor is responsible for you and to you.

Finding a good doctor can be time-consuming. Look for a doctor whom you trust (and hopefully like). If you feel that you are "rushed through," and no attention is paid to reasonable questions and requests for explanations, then you have the freedom to choose another doctor. Ask your friends' opinions. Your local medical society will give you doctors' names. Your hospital will have a list of doctors who are taking new patients.

1. Illness

When illness hits you, call your doctor. Reporting early symptoms will enhance better treatment. Don't ignore a new, significant pain and hope it will go away. Don't fail to tell your doctor about a bad dizzy spell, some blood in the urine, or any other unusual event. Don't diagnose yourself! That is your doctor's job.

Common illnesses occur most frequently. Good treatment is available for most of these conditions. If you have coughed up a bit of blood, the odds are that you have bronchitis. This is easily treated. Probably you don't have lung cancer or Chinese lung fluke infestation or some other bad disease. Fear of the worst makes some people stay away from the doctor.

Most fear that we experience is fear of the unknown. We human beings are a pretty tough lot and can face a lot of hard news without falling apart. We can accept a known illness with courage and fortitude. Panic comes in when symptoms remain undiagnosed and our imaginations go wild.

2. Drugs and medicines

"Self help" is quite acceptable if you are dealing with known minor conditions. "Over the counter" medicines are generally pretty safe. However, I want to make a few points about prescription drugs.

Prescription drugs are all potent and have a definite action on the body. Many have side effects even at the usual doses. You must obey some commonsense rules:

(a) Alcohol and drugs don't mix. Don't drink when you are taking any prescription drug.

(b) Make sure you clearly understand how many pills per day you should take. Don't change the dose without talking to your doctor.

(c) Ask your doctor about possible side effects. (You should be told this anyway.) If side effects occur, report them immediately.

(d) If you are a "doctor-hopper" (a most unwise practice) don't take two or three different drugs from two or three doctors.

It is amazing to me that some folks will visit two doctors for the same illness. Neither doctor knows this is happening. The two prescriptions are taken to different drug stores. What usually happens is that double doses of the same drug are taken. This is the road to disaster! You are certainly entitled to a second opinion about diagnosis and treatment. But don't confuse this basic right with "doctor-hopping."

(e) Sleeping pills and tranquilizers have their place in treatment; however, some doctors prescribe them for too long. Some patients demand them. I have lost many patients over the years because I wouldn't be a "good guy" and give a prescription for one of these drugs. It is reasonable to prescribe these drugs in many instances. However, it is not reasonable in many cases for a person to be "on a tranquilizer" for years just because they "feel better."

3. Doctor-patient problems

Many complaints are heard about doctors. Many are directed to medical societies. Sometimes lawyers are retained. In the majority of cases, the patient has never voiced the complaint to the doctor! Talk to the doctor first (not the secretary). If not satisfied, then of course, carry your complaint further.

Many complaints are due to lack of communication. Doctors and patients both have to improve these lines of communication. We are, after all, both trying for the same goal — to maintain your health or get you over an illness.

4. Conclusions

You as a patient have to take responsibility for your own health. A good doctor-patient relationship will enhance the quality of health care you receive.

17
MAKING YOUR FINAL PLAN

a. SET YOUR GOALS

Up to this point you have been examining parts of your life as if they were separate entities, but life is complex and consists of many parts and to work satisfactorily the parts must fit together to make a functioning unit. Now is the time to do this, to bring them together to plan a full, rounded, and satisfying life.

Success is most likely if there is a plan. Therefore, first decide what you really want in your retirement and then make a plan to achieve it. This is a very personal thing, no one else can know what is important or irrelevant to you. Decide what you would like to do or achieve. Include your fantasies for they may not be as farfetched as you fear, and only eliminate them later if they are crowded out or deemed not worth the cost. If equipment or training is required, set up a timetable for each phase to be sure it will be done.

Life is what you do as time passes; how you use that procession of moments determines how it can be evaluated. Therefore, begin your planning by thinking out how your time can be best spent. What will you do with the days so that at the end of each there will be a feeling of contentment? It need not all be classed as fun; part must be used for the requirements of living.

Your activities may be different from those of younger years, but so are your needs and goals. Change is not new with retirement, but has occurred with every stage of your life since birth.

Retirement is like turning off a crowded, high-speed freeway onto an unpaved country road. No longer must you strain to keep your place and watch the traffic. The tension fades away; you slow down. There is still much time, but it is not endless. Many avenues are now closed, but many new ones are opened. Your days are now entirely at your disposal.

b. THE NEW VALUE OF TIME

Time takes on a new value. During working years it was sold for the money to buy the necessities of life and its purchaser was often a hard task master who demanded full value. Now it takes on a new dimension — it has become the coin used to buy your pleasures and satisfactions because it is no longer needed to buy the goods and services. The means to purchase necessities was stored away over the years as pay deductions or savings and now returns as pension and investment income.

A new supply of time comes each day. It differs from money in that it cannot be stored but melts away like ice in the summer sun and if not spent upon arrival is lost forever. Could there be a more shameful waste than to permit life to melt away unused?

c. DO NOT BELIEVE IT!

There are many unfounded myths related to aging and to accept them could be a barrier to planning the best kind of life that is possible.

The first is that it is difficult to learn new things. How this arose no one knows, but ability in this respect is probably related to one's desires or attitude. If you want to learn, you can; it has been proven that the capability to do so remains as good as ever well into advanced age. Because of a wealth of experience, it may be possible for the older person to see concepts more readily and absorb them more quickly than when they were younger.

There is the problem of forgetfulness, which is really a slowness rather than an inability, for there is so much stored in the mind at this stage that it may take longer to sort through and recall the desired information. However, it seems to come back as well as ever after a short interval.

d. BE ACTIVE

Physical strength and energy does decline and it will impose restrictions. These are not as serious as in the past for there are so many mechanical aids to take the place of muscle: golf carts, ski lifts, the automobile, outboard motors, power lawn mowers, elevators, and all sorts of specialized equipment. Living accommodation on one floor or reached by elevators eliminates climbing stairs.

Have you noticed how few physically handicapped people there are compared to the number around when you were young? Medical care has prolonged good health and new surgical procedures revitalize many. As an example, that old crippler, the painful, worn out hip joint is now often completely replaced, which permits painless, normal movement.

Many people in the past suffered from what was frequently diagnosed as senility, but was simply a turning inward usually caused by living alone and losing touch with others and the world around them. Now that this is understood, it can be prevented by having a proper lifestyle, and often those who are in this position can be brought out of it by bringing them back into a suitable environment. People can remain normal into advanced old age.

e. LOVE CONTINUES

In past generations love and sex were never discussed publicly or in the media. There was much ignorance and misunderstanding, and it was feared that sexual activity would terminate at a relatively early age. Now these things are being investigated by qualified people and their findings publicized and more fully discussed. The indications are that sexual activity can continue into old age, probably at a reduced level, but still with as great a meaning and importance to human relationships as ever. A mutually satisfying love life can continue indefinitely if the partners wish it.

f. A LIFE WITH QUALITY

While some pleasures may be ruled out on the grounds of physical requirements, many others are available to replace them. It is foolish to feel that there is nothing left if certain cherished pastimes must end, for there are so many others to replace them that the prospect for enjoyment remains. There is the time to try, to sort out, and to choose. There are so many prospects and so many people available to help, and so many organizations offering special discounts, rights, and opportunities for the retired that everyone has the possibility of having a satisfying and rewarding life. It is, however, another example of taking the horse to water — the horse must drink, you cannot do it for it. Likewise, you must make the decisions and the effort yourself to grasp the opportunities.

No previous retiring generation has had the opportunity which is before you. On average, you are retiring while physically active and at an earlier age. You can look forward to a longer life span in better health and with greater financial security. You have handled more difficult periods in life than this, take advantage of this opportunity which you and your fellow retirees have prepared. Your future is largely in your hands; what you make of it is up to you!

APPENDIX 1

CHECKLIST FOR RETIRING

Prior preparation

1. Think about retirement and the changes it will bring.

2. Prepare your retirement life plan with your spouse if you have one.

3. Obtain all details respecting pensions and insurances (group, life, income maintenance, health and disability policies) offered through group plans at your place of employment. Know the benefits you are entitled to while employed there and the options open to you on leaving or retiring.

4. Examine details of personally owned life insurance and pension plans. Consider options offered by them. Do not delay finding these facts until retirement. They should be part of planning all your personal programs.

5. Estimate financial position in retirement and work toward any changes desired to increase income and/or decrease expenses.

6. Obtain birth or baptismal certificate if you do not have one.

7. Contact the Social Security Administration if you are 62 or older and plan to retire or if you are within 3 months of 65 even if you do not plan to retire then.

8. If you are age 65 or older, blind, or disabled with limited income, contact the Social Security Administration to ascertain if you are eligible for supplemental security income.

9. Discuss with your tax professional the tax consequences of your retirement income.

One year prior to retirement

10. Discuss with employer his or her policy respecting retirement, options for continued employment, and all benefits and options you may have.

On retirement

11. Meet with responsible officer at place of employment. Discuss again all benefits to which you are entitled. Be sure to get wages, holiday pay, and any cash coming from company benefit plans.

12. Obtain list of any health, medical, and hospital plans that have been paid by employer but which you must now pay directly. Get instructions and forms and apply at once.

13. Obtain a list of any options you have respecting group insurance, pension, etc. Do not decide these in haste. Take information and decide carefully at home after receiving any advice you desire.

14. Have medical and dental examinations.

15. Both you and your spouse make or review wills.

16. Start quarterly income tax payments if necessary.

APPENDIX 2

RESOURCES FOR RETIRED PEOPLE

American Association of Retired Persons (AARP)
1909 K Street, N.W.
Washington, D.C. 20049
Telephone: (202)872-4700

Area Agencies on Aging (AAA)
Consult the local government section of your telephone directory

Elderhostel
80 Boylston Street
Suite 400
Boston, Massachusetts 02116

National Association for Home Care
519 C Street, N.E.
Washington, D.C. 20002

Social Security Administration
Telephone toll-free: 1-800-937-2000

National Academy of Elder Law Attorneys, Inc.
135 S.W. Ash Street
Suite 500
Portland, Oregon 97204

OTHER TITLES IN THE SELF-COUNSEL RETIREMENT SERIES

MARGO OLIVER'S COOKBOOK FOR SENIORS
Nutritious recipes for one — two — or more
by Margo Oliver

Cooking Expert Margo Oliver presents appetizing recipes along with useful kitchen know-how in this book designed especially for seniors. In her personal style, she addresses some of the special concerns of mature adults while keeping the flavor in the food.

Whether you are a novice or experienced cook, whether you are cooking for yourself or more, you'll find these recipes — over 150 — interesting and fun to make. $9.95

Contents include:

- Kitchen helpers
- Know-how for new cooks
- Appetizers, Snacks, and Sips
- Soups and Sauces
- Main Dishes
- Salads and Vegetables
- Breads and Cereals
- Sweets
- Suggested Menus
- Index

MOBILE RETIREMENT HANDBOOK
A complete guide to living and traveling in an RV
by Jurgen Hesse

The author provides many helpful tips on choosing the right RV, drawing up a budget for both money and time, preparing to leave your home, and organizing a network of friends while you're on the road.

"*This handbook will answer your questions on whether retirement in an RV is right for you. Anyone contemplating the pleasures of this lifestyle should have this book.*"
John Gedak, President, Get-Away Enterprises Inc.
$9.95

Contents include

- Leaving your dream home
- Choosing the right RV
- Operating and maintaining an RV
- Shutting down your base
- What to take along
- Masterminding your getaway
- Where will you go?
- Foreign destinations
- Behavior on the road
- Safety on the road
- Finding good campsites
- Keeping busy on the road

WISE AND HEALTHY LIVING
A commonsense approach to aging well
by Richard D. Underwood and
Brenda Breeden Underwood

Retirement years can be full of activity and happy times if approached with a positive attitude and a willingness to make minor changes to adapt to changing physical and psychological needs. This book presents a holistic approach to aging and health. It discusses the aging process and the changes to be expected, how to deal with change, and how it may affect the way you live. $8.95

FIT AFTER FIFTY
Feel better Live longer
by Dr. Roy J. Shephard and Dr. Scott G. Thomas

This book explains the importance of exercise, the effects of aging on how you exercise, how to exercise, precautions to take, special considerations for those with particular health problems, and perhaps most important, the great variety of enjoyable activities that qualify as exercise. $8.95

ORDER FORM

All prices subject to change without notice. Books are available in book and department stores. If you cannot buy the book through a store, please use this order form. (Please print)

Name _____

Address _____

_____

Charge to:

    ❑ Visa   ❑ MasterCard

Account Number _____

Validation Date _____ Expiry Date _____

Signature _____

❑ **Check here for a free catalog outlining all of our publications.**

Please send your order to:
Self-Counsel Press Inc.
1704 N. State Street
Bellingham, WA 98225

Yes, please send me:

_____ copies of MARGO OLIVER'S COOKBOOK FOR SENIORS, $9.95

_____ copies of MOBILE RETIREMENT HANDBOOK, $9.95

_____ copies of WISE AND HEALTHY LIVING $8.95

_____ copies of FIT AFTER FIFTY, $8.95

There is a $2.50 charge for postage and handling.

Washington residents please add 7.8% sales tax.